Of The First Magnitude

~I~

~Volume 1~
Facing Revelation
An Emerging

~Volume 2~
iRise
An Algorhythm of Freedom

~Volume 3~
Quantum Engineering
Introspecting the Rabbit Hole

~Volume 4~
Algorhythmic Insight
Poetic Analysis of the Journey

Copyright Notice:

Read it!

Integrate it!

Live it!

Truth, that is...

© 2017, 2022 – Michael J.M. Phoenix - All Rights Reserved. All rights reserved. No part of this publication may be reproduced, distributed, or transmitted in any form or by any means, including photocopying, recording, or other electronic or mechanical methods, without the prior written permission of the publisher, except in the case of brief quotations embodied in critical reviews and certain other noncommercial uses permitted by copyright law.

For permission requests, write to the publisher, addressed "Attention: Permissions Coordinator," at the address below.

Emergent Strategies LLC
PO Box 245
Winona, MO. 65588

https://3m3r3g.com
orders@3m3rg3.com

ISBN: 978-1-7337454-1-3

Cover Art: Sam Whelan - https://www.samwhelan.net/

~ Volume 2 ~

iRise

An Algorhythm of Freedom

By Michael Phoenix

"You are the light of the world…"
-Yeshua the Christ

Overview

INROADS	10
CONTEXTUAL PREMISE	13
INTRODUCTION	17
Reasons	17
A Word of Warning	19
ARTICLE 1	23
Foundation	23
CHAPTER 1	24
Metaphysical Axiom	24
I Am	24
Pillar of Existence	25
Pillar of Consciousness	32
Pillar of Infinity	33
Pillar of Unconditional Love	35
CHAPTER 2	40
Epistemological Axiom	40
I Am Light	40
The Empire of Rational Knowledge	45
Objectivity	48
Subjectivity	49
Unconditional Love	52
CHAPTER 3	57
Ethical Axiom	57
I Am Integrity	57
Two Methods of Experience	59
Dying in Dishonesty	60
Living with Integrity	61
CHAPTER 4	64
Aesthetical Axiom	64
I Am Life	64
The World as a Mirror	65

Value Deflection	67
Value Reflection	69

CHAPTER 5 — 73

Political Axiom	73
I Am Creator	73
World of Fear	74
World of Love	77
Bridges out of the World of Fear	78
Bridge Into the World of Love	82

ARTICLE 2 — 89

Dynamics 89

CHAPTER 1 — 90

Movement: Sloth to Integrity	90
Sloth	90
Integrity	93

CHAPTER 2 — 97

Movement: Greed to Abundance	97
Greed	97
Abundance	99

CHAPTER 3 — 104

Movement: Wrath to Power	104
Wrath	104
Power	107

CHAPTER 4 — 111

Movement: Envy to Honor	111
Envy	111
Honor	112

CHAPTER 5 — 115

Movement: Lust to Sex	115
Lust	115
Sex	118

CHAPTER 6 — 123

Movement: The Choice	123

    Choose With Wisdom   123

ARTICLE 3 — 127

    Process   127

CHAPTER 1 — 128

Method: Concentration	128
Managing the Attention Point	128
Center Point of the Mind	129
Exercise 1: Centering in the Brain	130
Exercise 2: Pyramid of Negative Space	132
Exercise 3: Octahedron Mind Space	132

CHAPTER 2 — 134

Method: Contemplation	134
Clear Thinking	134
Clear Feeling	135
Clear Sensing	137
Synergizing the Functions	139
Exercise 1: Centering Self	140
Exercise 2: Refactoring Questions	140
Exercise 3: Daily Permutations	141

CHAPTER 3 — 143

Method: Meditation	143
Observation	143
Active Observation	143
Passive Observation	144
Exercise 1: The Flame of Integrity (Active)	145
Exercise 2a: The Flower (Active & Passive)	146
Exercise 2b: The Christ Flower (Active & Passive)	146
Exercise 3: Trinity Expression (Passive)	147

CHAPTER 4 — 149

Method: Introspection	149
Orienting the Internal Map	149
Exercise 1: Whom Do I Truly Serve?	151
Exercise 2: Who Am I?	152

CHAPTER 5 — 153

    Method: Integration   153
    Integrating Breath   153
    Integrating Body   154
    Integrating Mind   154
    Integrating Emotion   155
    Integrating Spirit   157
    Exercise 1: Breath Integration   158
    Exercise 2: Body Integration   159
    Exercise 3: Mind Integration   160
    Exercise 4: Emotion Integration   161
    Exercise 5: Spirit Integration   163

ARTICLE 4   164

    Truth   164

CHAPTER 1   165

    Yahweh   165
    To Conceive   165

CHAPTER 2   168

    Yeshua   168
    An Appeal to Reason   168
    Jesus: The Story   169
    Jesus: The Man   171
    Jesus: The Messiah   172
    Jesus: The Christ   173

CHAPTER 3   175

    You   175
    Ego   175
    Who Am I   178

CHAPTER 4   180

    Reclaiming the Earth   180
    The Life of a Rastafarian Druid: Spreading the Love   180

CHAPTER 5   183

    Becoming The Christ   183
    The Indwelling   183
    Forgiveness   184

Everliving Freedom	185	

CHAPTER 6 — 187

The Fallacy of Religion	187
Loving Yourself	187

CHAPTER 7 — 190

Union through Sex	190
For the Mathematicians Among Us	190

CHAPTER 8 — 195

On {this} Philosophy	195
For the Philosophers Among Us	195

OTHER TITLES BY MICHAEL PHOENIX — 198

Inroads

Journey Within…
Reveal Truth…
Be Free…

The six-word phrase above is a summation of the breadth and scope of the reality conveyed through the words in this book. This algorithm typifies a series of movements that act as a function of consciousness, where you, the user, can begin to reprogram your consciousness toward a synergy with the fundamental fabric of existence.

Regardless of where you currently find yourself in life, and the journey that has led you to this point, I invite you to take all your ideas about who you *think* you are, and set them aside while you embrace this book. The more you set aside who you think you are, and *allow* the actuality of who you really are to present itself, the less you need this book, or any other book.

As it is, this book presents you with a philosophy; a set of ideas. It is only a philosophy, a thinking strategy. **It is not something you must adopt and make yourself a slave to. It is not something that answers all questions. And it is not something to regard as right or wrong.** Whether you agree with it is of no real concern. You experiencing the reality of life that this book *points* to, that is *of the first magnitude* – **the highest priority**. The *first* and *final* movement.

You need not believe everything this book offers, as I said, your belief is not necessary. What matters most is that *you* open yourself to the reality of the inner communion with the primal cause of all reality (in this book, the label designated to that primal cause is "Creator").

There is no philosophy, idea, or belief that will ever hold the degree of real value inherent to the living source of all existence. To be clear, eventually, **you will need to let go of all *your* ideas in order**

to attain that full communion – I'm simply encouraging you to do so now, here, in this very instant. The Reality of life is ever present and does not need interpretation to be real. It is our duty to lay aside all that stands in the way of fully embracing that which is the prime root of our very existence, in this instant. In the moment you do this, you will open channels of light within yourself that will forever alter the reality of your disposition in life – your paradigm.

There is no idea as significant as the Idea that is the living Creator, the Absolute standard upon which all existence derives it necessary origination – and you are an extension of that living Creator. Created by that Creator as perfect in your truest essence – your prime root.

To assume that the Creator made a mistake by creating the primal qualitative and quantitative constructs that pre-dispose you to the energetic capacity for personality extension, i.e. Your existence, and that you are inherently flawed, assumes that the Creator makes mistakes. The constancy of your innocence is as constant as this moment – it exists without question. Thus, **your significance in existence must *never* be under-estimated.**

In the vastness that is universal reality, the home you have never left, where all life is awaiting your arrival, is in the very center of your Being – Your Heart. When you awaken to this truth, you will know a level of concord that passes understanding.

This is not some airy-fairy ideological pipe dream. Do not confuse yourself. Do not delude yourself. The suffering that you have endured in your life need not go in vain. In every moment you open your heart to the pain and suffering you *feel* inside and *see* outside, you open the healing waters of spirit to come in and nourish your soul's existence, *and move you one step closer to home.* Please re-read this paragraph; it conveys the nature of the journey you have found yourself taking. Vulnerability is Power.

The deeper the commitment you have, the quicker the revealing. **Be warned**, however, in this revealing you will meet face-to-face all the demons, false notions, and lies that you have harbored. Again, where you place your attention point, your commitment, your focus – this will determine the ease with which you release that which is of no use, and embrace that which is.

Remember, when you reach the doorway of significance, you are not a self-created entity with an independent existence; you are a unique emanation effulging from the primal substance that permeates all existence simultaneously; you may call it love if you wish. Knock and the door shall open.

Contextual Premise

> The Most important one is this: "Hear, O Israel: The Lord our God, the Lord is *One*. Love the Lord your God with all your heart and with all your soul and with all your mind and with all your strength." The second is this: "Love your neighbor as yourself." There is no commandment greater than these.
>
> Yeshua

This passage of text arrives to us through a dialogue Yeshua Ben Yosef, the anointed Christos from Nazareth, more commonly known as Jesus of Nazareth, had with a teacher-of-the-law during the days he walked the earth of the first coming.

As it pertains to law, it is assumed that *law* is an order of *conduct*; an injunction. Just as a law stipulates that a green light is a signal for a motorist to "go", the two most important of all laws is to Love the One Lord and to love your neighbor as yourself. The Light is Green – GO!

Now let us contemplate, who is the One Lord?

> Now there were seven brothers. The first one married and died without leaving any children. The second one married the widow, but he also died, leaving no child. It was the same with the third. In fact, none of the seven left any children. Last of all, the woman died too. At the resurrection whose wife will she be, since the seven were married to her?
>
> Jesus replied, "Are you not in error because you do not know the Scriptures, or the power of God? When the dead rise, they will neither marry nor be given in marriage; they will be like the angels in heaven. Now about the dead rising—have you not read in the Book of Moses, in the account of

the burning bush, how God said to him, 'I am the God of Abraham, the God of Isaac, and the God of Jacob'? He is not the God of the dead, **but of the living**. You are badly mistaken! [emphasis added]

The Apostle Mark

As it is plainly spoken by Yeshua, the Master Teacher; God, is a God (Primary Causation) of the *living*. Indeed, it is, A is A. Existence is *existing*.

And as it pertains to *law*, what is law other than an instruction *to do*? Where does one derive the authority upon which the doing assimilates the nature and premise of the given authority? If an individual only engages in an effort of doing, and never enters into a full integration of the *being* that is the *necessary basis* of the doing, the doing will remain only on superficial levels of integration. Whereas, if the doing is a full derivative issuing forth from total integration of the premise from which the law finds its authoritative justification, the doing takes its natural course and is the effect of the primary cause of being.

As it is instructed, *the motive is to love*. To whom am I to extend love to? God and our neighbors. How am I to extend that love? With my whole heart, mind, soul and strength. With everything that is "me"!

Let us further clarify the terms "God" and "neighbors" so as to create a clear space of communication. As defined **herein**, when looking at the context of experiential life, "God" is a three-letter word referring to the creative intelligent impulse that sustains all of existence from an infinite past to an infinite future, and expresses through experience here in the present moment. Qualitatively, the character traits are omnipresent, omnipotent, and omniscient. "Neighbors" is a nine-letter word referring to all fields of energy observable as identifiable self-aware sentient objects in the space-time construct.

For the one who *sees* this plainly and *does* as instructed, this book is only a summary of what is already known. For the one who still experiences inner and outer conflict to any degree, this book may be of use.

As it is, anyone who participates in regular society to any extent has a high degree of probability towards experiencing external conflict. As identified by the premises espoused in this book, the cause of the external dissonance stems from a state of internal dissonance within the individuals experiencing external dissonance – inner conflict begets world conflict. And likewise, inner peace begets world peace. Until the point that this planet reaches a maximal interaction of individuals existing in balance and synergy with one another, conflict is present, and resistance is its call sign.

To that end, it is the inner harmony that resonates throughout ones being that aligns a group of individuals into a maximal synergistic output. The journey of inner harmony is always an individual pursuit and must be freely chosen *by* the individual who wishes to resonate in the alignment of the primary motive – *to love!*

The journey through which this book offers its contextual framework and associated tools is framed by the recognition that the exterior environment perceived is a mirror of the interior environment constructed; in this, these tools arrive at their efficacy.

The second most important injunction is to "Love your neighbor as yourself." In deed that sounds noble. Yet, the application of that order may not be so feasible when there is no *applicable* knowledge of true Self.

The question to contemplate with is as follows: "Who is self? If I am to love my neighbor as myself, I must first love myself. But what is it to love myself?" The intention of this book is to answer that question, not necessarily through direct testimony, but more so through inquiry, introspection and direct experience, by you, the reader.

The most fundamental aspect to keep in mind while reading this book is the definition of religion espoused herein. This definition is not found in any dictionary, is counter to the predominant notions of religion, and is entirely surmised through the processes outlined in this book – **Religion**: an individual experience in the achievement of consciously integrating in a spiritual relationship with the causal nature of reality.

Introduction

Reasons

Revelation, in its function, is when a soul opens into that which is beyond form; an awakening into Spiritual Reality where Truth is *known* and questions of doubt are a nonexistent concept. The tribulations that arise on the journey of revelation present themselves as opportunities to more fundamentally unite with the inner reality – the basic nature of existence:

> If you love me, keep my commands. And I will ask the Father, and he will give you another advocate to help you and be with you forever – the Spirit of truth. The world cannot accept him, because it neither sees him nor knows him. But you know him, for he lives with you and **will be in you**. [emphasis added]
>
> Yeshua

The effect of the journey that this book points to, arrives at the destination of freedom – "and the Truth shall set you free". The journey begins with awareness.

As it pertains to the journey, there is no single path that is set out as a template for everyone. Each individual walks a unique path.

There is; however, a set of meta-processes at work. These processes, or functions, serve as principles – a unifying application of consciousness.

As was said above, the destination is freedom. Freedom is a natural effect after the fifth and final application, at which point, light is given its space to shine.

For a soul that has been inundated with a degree of density sufficient enough to obscure the radiation of light from transmitting cleanly through the cosmic construct that is the soul, it is the application of this algorithm that bestows freedom; thus, this algorithm derives its name – The Algorhythm of Freedom.

Freedom is the purpose. Upon realization of freedom, the algorithm integrates as a way of being. That is to say, through the application of a set of functions that arrive at freedom, the functions attain a relationship of synergy in which they become a natural mode of living.

Freedom is the choice in any given context. When the *embodiment* of freedom is not functioning, this algorithm can be set in motion. This is a process of ascension, moving from one level of awareness into a higher, more integrated level of awareness. It is as a boy growing into a man, he ascends in his mastery of responsibility – his ability to respond to life. This ascension requires an ever-increasing mastery in the responsiveness to awareness.

The algorithm is as follows: Awareness to Willingness to Openness to Honesty to Transparency. The destination is transparent expression of self – Freedom.

Each function sequentially follows one after another in every instance the algorithm is initiated. It is *initiated* between awareness and willingness.

Becoming aware of aspects of existence often happens as a random input of information, wherein the output may or may not lead to awareness. However, when the light of awareness has flashed, *choice* is at hand.

In every moment the algorithm is applied, it is the choice in *willingness* that performs the processing of the function. Willingness to be willing. Willingness to be open. Willingness to be honest. Willingness to be transparent.

Each sub-routine is called by the choice to be willing. When the will is extended, the process of that permutation proceeds naturally, and in due course, completes upon realization of the destination that is Freedom.

Awareness is seeing, feeling, and sensing the fullest possible scope of the given situation in present time.

Willingness functions as a choice to process the information; it is saying "Yes" to all that life has to offer – the pain and the pleasure.

Openness is being willing to fully *receive* the information of Light as an input.

Honesty is being willing to act in alignment with discernment of that information.

Transparency is being willing to let the light of that information shine through as an output, as an expression.

The effect of all this is the *embodiment of freedom*. This character trait demonstrates as *integrity*. A virtue of wisdom.

Every aspect of this set of functions provides necessary reason to walk the journey. In every instance that a choice is made to further the progression of this ever-increasing spiral of *maturity*, it serves the growth and evolution of the individual, as well as the collective. In the One Lord (the causal nature of reality), there is no disconnect. Alignment to the One Lord is through the activation of the highest injunction – to love.

This process is revelation.

Proceed at your choice...

A Word of Warning

The path that you have embarked upon is not a path for the faint of heart. If you are easily swayed from your convictions, this path is NOT for you.

This path is ONLY for those who have completely turned over their life to living in communion with the Creator – in every thought, every breath, every word, and every action. If you are not at this level of commitment, you will need to be before you can fully comprehend the efficacy of what this book is pointing to.

In that, you are **expected** to test this.

How do you test this?

If you consider yourself a disciple of Christ, meaning, you are someone who listens to the Master's words and applies those precepts in your life, please, go get your bible and open the book to 1 John 4. *Do* that now!

For the remainder of this book, as I have written it, I have operated from the assumption that you have read that chapter.

Why is this pertinent?

It is pertinent because A is A.

What does that mean? It means that Truth is Truth.

When I speak of Truth I am speaking of the absolute; that which is beyond reproach – Perfection.

1 John 4 illustrates this with the following:

> There is no fear in love, but perfect love casts out fear. For fear has to do with punishment, and whoever fears has not been perfected in love. We love because he first loved us. If anyone says, "I love God," and hates his brother, he is a liar; for he who does not love his brother whom he has seen cannot love God whom he has not seen. And this commandment we have from him: whoever loves God must also love his brother.
>
> The Apostle John

In our pursuit to enter into divine communion with the Creator, the preeminent command we have is to give our hearts, our minds, and our souls in an effort that is at the maximal output of our strength. In doing this we not only love ourselves; we love God and our neighbor – courage is a prerequisite in this process of ascension.

As you read this book, you may come to the safety of Truth through the purification of your soul that is administered by the revealing light of the Creator's primal energy – unending love and unceasing light – in a word, Grace.

If you sense fear, or any form of it in yourself, you must come to look at that impurity within yourself and willingly bring it to the altar of Truth as a sacrifice of *surrender* in order to deepen your commitment in your relationship with the Creator – this beast must be cast into the abyss – false notions must be clarified.

It is not for you to hold onto your fears out of a selfish attachment to your beliefs. It is for you to let go of everything that keeps you from knowing the Creator in its entire splendor. Every facet of Truth. Every function of Consciousness. Every ability in Spirit. Here, now, in this domain of life.

Being a disciple of Christ is a noble adventure. **Your clinging to fears is not permitted.** In all the ways that you doubt, you must relinquish this doubt to come into a full spectrum relationship with your divinity – this may quite literally feel like hell at points[1].

You cannot assume you *know* Truth when you experience a clinging to doubt and fear in any way. In every moment where you experience doubt and fear, you must make the decision to consciously recognize the opportunity before you and present yourself in vulnerability to your Godhead, the source of your existence. In this presentation you must be absolute in your willingness to surrender your false ideas and replace them with full honesty.

This is the journey.

---

[1] Understand that you are in the process of deconstructing every false notion that you hold about yourself. Some of these notions/concepts have been with you since birth. When you destroy a false notion, there will inevitably be fear, as you have no conception of what's beyond that false notion. This reasoning is the underlying premise that justifies the fact that *faith* is a necessity on this journey. Begin to be "okay" with the fact that you have no clue what this journey will present to you.

This is the quest.
There is no turning back!

Article 1

Foundation

1: The Tao that can be trodden is not the enduring and unchanging Tao. The name that can be named is not the enduring and unchanging name. Having no name it is the Originator of heaven and Earth; having a name, it is the Mother of all things. Always without desire we must be found, If its deep mystery we would wound; But if desire always within us be, Its outer fringe is all that we shall see. Under these two aspects, it is really the same; but as development takes place, it receives the different names. Together we call them the Mystery. Where the Mystery is the deepest is the gate of all that is subtle and wonderful.

2: All in the world know the beauty of the beautiful, and in doing this they have what ugliness is; they all know the skill of the skillful, and in doing this they have what the want of skill is. So it is that existence and non-existence give birth the one to the other; that difficulty and ease produce the one to the other; that length and shortness fashion out the one the figure of the other; that height and lowness arise from the contrast of the one with the other; that the musical notes and tones become harmonious through the relation of one with another; and that being before and behind give the idea of one following another.

10: When the intelligent and animal souls are held together in one embrace, they can be kept from separating. When one gives undivided attention to the breath, and brings it to the utmost degree of pliancy, he can become as a babe. When he has cleansed away the most mysterious sights, he can become without a flaw. In loving the people and ruling the state, cannot he proceed without any action? In the opening and shutting of his gates of heaven, cannot he do so as a female bird? While his intelligence reaches in every direction, cannot he be without knowledge? The Tao produces all things and nourishes them; it produces them and does not claim them as its own; it does all, and yet does not boast of it; it presides over all and yet does not control them. This is what is called 'The mysterious Quality' of the Tao.

Tao Te Ching verses 1,2 & 10

Chapter 1

Metaphysical Axiom

That which is *meta* to the physical does *not* necessarily delineate the specificity of that which is the physical construction – it holds the archetypal pattern. The meta-physical is that which establishes the *sustaining ability* to exist in the present moment. The meta-pattern of personality.

I Am

If a presence of existing effulgence[2] pre-dominates the rational capacity of observation, then also present is the awareness of life. Presence denotes a quality of being aware in the present tense. Existing effulgence denotes a current quality of a certain quantity of radiating substance.

If, in the observational awareness of an entity, this presence of existing effulgence is internally focused, then the base identification is *I Am*. This identification is founded in being aware of a basic level of awareness, "I am aware that I am aware." Furthermore, there is no moment that an individual cannot make this identification.

The identification of "I" is an awareness of one's individual frame of reference. The identification of "Am" is the awareness of the fact that the frame currently exists in the present moment.

A mind with the capacity to retain awareness in the focus of reading these words is a mind with the capacity to recognize this presence of that which is "I Am". Only ignorance can remain oblivious to the reality of this basic degree of awareness. But where does this

---

[2] Effulgence: radiance; the quality of being bright and sending out rays of light.

basic degree of awareness stem from? Is this awareness generated only as an effect from an organic machine known as the brain? Or does the brain not take part in the generation of awareness, but only processes the information that stems from awareness?

In either case, there is currently a motion of awareness directed by the decision of the individual reading these words to continue reading these words. Thus, in reality, there is no possibility to *not* identify one's self; therefore, the most basic identification that can be made by the individual who is choosing to read these words is *I exist*. Another way to declare that statement is – I Am.

> But Moses said to God, "Who *am* I that I should go to Pharaoh, and that I should bring the children of Israel out of Egypt?" So He said, "I will certainly be with you. And this *shall be* a sign to you that I have sent you: When you have brought the people out of Egypt, you shall serve God on this mountain."
>
> Then Moses said to God, "Indeed, *when* I come to the children of Israel and say to them, "The God of your fathers has sent me to you,' and they say to me, 'What *is* His name?' what shall I say to them?
>
> And God said to Moses, "I AM WHO I AM." And He said, "Thus you shall say to the children of Israel, 'I AM has sent me to you.'"
>
> Exodus 3:11-14

Pillar of Existence

Awareness *is*, and this is proven by the fact that there is an awareness observing these words. Abstracting to a more encompassing perspective in awareness, it is observed that there is an awareness of being aware of these words; observing the observer, as it were. But what is the basic substance of existence that allows for the possibility of a human being to have the opportunity to be aware of being aware?

According to scientific inquiry, there are certain forces that guide the fundamental nature of how things interact at an essential physical level. Without these forces, the universe as it currently exists simply would not exist. The *Laws of Physics* are an integral way in which the modern mind understands and orients to life.

And yet, in a metaphysical approach to recognize the nature of reality, the mind approaches the meta-physical forces. In that approach, the mind engages forces that are beyond physically perceivable forms or identifiable structures; that which is *meta* to the physical universe. And although the forces are meta to the physical, they are still very much entwined with how the physical operates.

To metaphysically reason is to engage the mind in highly abstract thoughts, concepts and ideas, such as infinity and eternity. Contemplation[3] is a mode through which the mind metaphysically reasons.

The contemplative angle of inquiry about sensation, perception, and reality is as follows; does the spirit of a human exist as the foundation for the body of that same human, or does the body of the human exist as the sole progenitor of that human's existence? Which is the more prime construct, the spirit, or the body?

Further down this line of inquiry, the journey inevitably leads to the question of the mind, what it is, where it stems from, how it operates, etc. At the heart of the dilemma is the question of whether

---

[3] Contemplation: the act of feeling the effect of thoughts with the purpose of integrating an operational way of being that is in line with an open heart. The premise behind this definition of contemplation speaks to a principled way of living life wherein an individual moves with the intention to dissolve all mental irrationality and disintegrate all emotional rigidity; the effect of which is an open mind and an open heart. The purpose of an open mind and heart is to freely allow the basic substance of the universe to flow through without impeding it. In this treatment of metaphysics, another phrase to describe the basic substance of the universe is *unconditional love*.

mind is a universal principle that exists independent of a body that can harness it, or if the brain and its network of sensory mechanisms in the body is the generating mechanism for mind? In other words, does mind have a location, or does it permeate the entirety of existence?

There is no easy answer to these questions, and in the end, it is up to each individual to plunge into the depth of existence and directly experience the reality of that which answers these questions in finality. Because, *in the end*, it is the journey itself that reveals the abstract in the concrete.

And in terms of revealing the abstract in the concrete, consider for a moment the concept of "human". The concept "human" is an abstraction in relation to a specific or concrete individual. Human is a general term that defines a certain type of mammal, just as "dog" is an abstraction that is a general term for another type of mammal. The term "mammal" is even more abstract than dog or human. Creature is even more abstract than mammal. And "spirit" is still more abstract than creature. The term "energy" is on a level of abstraction that is near "spirit". The point of contemplation in all of this is, is it possible to directly observe spirit? And likewise, is it possible to directly observe energy?

The assertion may be made that one can observe the *movements* or *influence* of energy, such as a car traveling down a road. There is force of energy that exerts, an influence giving the vehicle its locomotion. But is it possible to *directly* observe the actual substance that gives rise to the movement? Again, the assertion can be made that gasoline is that energy. Yet, what is *it* that gives gasoline its ability to exist? What is the source of energy that lives as the explosive potential of gasoline?

Take gravity for instance, is the force field of gravity perceptible to the visual sense? Or, is it more accurate to say that gravity is detectable because its influence on matter can be seen by the way it interacts with the visible objects it comes into relationship with?

The physical processes of perception detect form and structure. Looking at this book, the mind sees word forms or symbols. Words are composed of letters, and letters are lines constructed with certain directions – up, down, left, right, etc.

Contemplation is an act of engaging the mind *and* heart in a continued focus of attention towards an awareness of that which exists as the framework of perceivable structures; that which is *meta* to the physical reality. If a practitioner of contemplation were to observe from a central location inside the body, noticing the energy radiating itself presently, it can then be identified that every perceivable thing is sourced from this energy.

The term energy, as it is applied here, is a general term indicating the presence of a stable substance with the qualities necessary to predicate life activity. The phrase "life activity" assumes a quality of existence and action. The word "life" assumes a sense of existing and the word "activity" assumes a dynamic tendency. These words are representative of *concepts*. The concepts are representative of *experiences*. That is to say, in order for a concept to represent an experience, there must be an existing reality that holds the potential for that existing reality to stabilize as a kinetic construct.

For example, a sense of the energy known as *momentum* can be experienced by riding a roller coaster. A sense of the energy of light can be experienced by observing the sun. The subtle, but critical, distinction being made is that the substance underlying the force of momentum and the radiance of light exists as a *meta*-construct to physical reality.

Energy, in its many forms, is present everywhere. It is even present in a dormant form known as potential energy. There is a potential to discontinue reading. Yet, that potential remains dormant so long as reading continues. Both are directions of movement, reading or not reading. And every*thing* in the universe is in constant movement. In a sense, this ever-persistent movement is a radiation of the underlying energy that provides the substance that gives rise to the circuitry of life activity.

The radiating effect that occurs is understandable with the concept of a "ray". A ray, in geometrical terms, has a source point with a line of propagation that continues without end. A sentient being with self-awareness is a source point in-and-of-itself in that it can make a choice to look and move in any direction – a being of sentience has the power of will.

A sentient being can make the decision to read this book, or not. The fundamental nature of the geometry of life for an individual person is such that every decision acts as an expression of the radiant energy that is awareness. Light, as in light from the sun, and awareness, as in awareness within oneself, act very much the same. *They both reveal.* Sunlight reveals what is on the earth. Awareness reveals what is in oneself.

Recognizing the fundamental nature of the reality of awareness aligns one's mind to the most basic actuality known as "Life" – *awareness is present, and it shines as light.* This geometry is the sacred allocation of all real information. Awareness shines forth from a central point within oneself. This light of awareness is not external moving inward, it is internal moving outward. Anything that does not attune to this sacred geometry is a source of information that is not true at its basis. All information that is not true is not real, thus, it has no life.

The Pillar of Existence says that anything that is true is real, all else is false and has no bearing on existence. The only place falsity has is the place an individual of sentience gives it in the mind. Accepting false assumptions to be true is to place an idol on the altar of the mind and to worship that idol with one's heart.

When an individual thinks, the mind's attention point focuses on the thought and that thought resonates with a certain frequency. This process produces certain physiological responses that can be felt.

Even now, while reading these words, the mind is being given over to the ideas contained in this book. The attention point is focusing the light of awareness on these words and the ideas are generating certain thoughts in the mind. As the mind thinks these thoughts, a field is generated creating a flow of energy that is aligned to the resonance of the thoughts contained herein. To consider these thoughts without accepting them outright is the key to the contemplative journey articulated herein. To simply accept another man's words without sincere contemplative consideration is a form of mental slavery – this beast must be slain.

All of life activity is happening both in the physical and the metaphysical. A thought, as it moves through the mind, is a metaphysical construct. The thought itself has a certain structure, but it does not have a solid physical state that can be directly observed, although its effects may be visible. More accurately, a thought could be described as non-physical energy that exerts influence on the physical world.

Can a thought be held in the hands, or does it move into awareness and move out of awareness? Where did the thought go? Does it exist as a piece of paper in a filing cabinet, or is it now a memory stored as a pattern of neuronal activity associated to a specific resonance of energy?

The word energy is an ambiguous symbol; ambiguous meaning it can refer to more than one thing. What is energy? Where does it originate? Where does it go? Is it created or destroyed, or does it get conserved such that it is neither created nor destroyed? If it is neither created nor destroyed, where did it come from? Has it always existed from an eternal past? Will it continue to exist into an eternal future? Are there more subtle forms of energy that exist beyond the ability of the physical senses to perceive? Are there more subtle forms of energy that exist beyond what modern scientific instruments can detect? What happens to the energy of awareness upon the ceasing of the physical body as a container for that awareness? Does awareness too get conserved in some form? Is there a survival of the personality in some form?

These questions are not meant to be answered directly by the rational mind, they are tools used for contemplation towards a deeper awareness of the metaphysical nature of reality. The question itself does not necessarily matter. It is a *curiosity* towards the direction the question points to that are most revealing. Forming conclusions as fact breaks the function of contemplation. In the place where the question is asked, the answer is present, but it is not only a process of rational thinking. It is also a process of opening the mind and engaging the heart in the effort to willingly receive an infusion of light that *moves through one's being,* from the internal to the external; such that knowledge is not knowledge unless it is given.

> There was a man of the Pharisees named Nicodemus, a ruler of the Jews. This man came to Jesus by night and said to Him, "Rabbi, we know that You are a teacher come from God; for no one can do these signs that You do unless God is with him."
>
> Jesus answered and said to him, "Most assuredly, I say to you, unless one is born again, he cannot see the kingdom of God."
>
> Nicodemus said to Him, "How can a man be born when his old? Can he enter a second time into his mother's womb and be born?"
>
> Jesus answered, "Most assuredly, I say to you, unless one is born of water and the Spirit, he cannot enter the kingdom of God. That which is born of the flesh is flesh, and that which is born of the Spirit is spirit. Do not marvel that I said to you, 'You must be born again.' **The wind blows where it wants, and you hear the sound thereof, but cannot tell**

> **from where it comes, and where it goes: so is every one that is born of the Spirit.** [emphasis added]
>
> The Apostle John

Pillar of Consciousness

The electrical impulse of every thought has a magnetic effect. The magnetic effect presents itself as a feeling. High electric charge in the body produces a feeling of excitement. The electric and magnetic energy that runs through and permeates the body is a radiant energy that reaches beyond the parameters of the physical human body. Just as the magnetic field of a magnet encompasses a space larger than the physical orientation of the material that composes the magnet, so too does the magnetic field produced by thought. This can be sensed from a feeling place, by one who is acutely aware of the subtlety of thought patterns.

Thinking certain thoughts, without taking any other action creates a magnetic resonance in the space around the source point. As the mind thinks, it originates a thought pattern, a form or wave of energy. This energy emits outward.

The brain's electro-chemical processes act as a generator of a specific vibration of energy. The higher the vibration, the higher the magnetic capacity. The higher the magnetic capacity, the higher degree of radiant intensity and expression.

The heart acts as an amplifier and transmitter. The brain focuses the light of attention into the heart which then amplifies and transmits that energy. Any thought that cannot access the higher vibratory patterns of the heart is a thought that is not aligned with Truth.

As it is, God is Love. The heart is an instrument that is specific to this function – Loving. Contemplation is the act of distilling the mental processes to a balance point with the heart wherein a synergy emerges.

Thoughts exist in certain vibratory rates and patterns. Thoughts that tune one's heart to happiness, beauty, joy and love are thoughts that align one's soul to Truth.

God is Love.

A is A.

Be warned, however, the residual decay that remains as the stagnant energy of suffering must be cleansed. To delude the mind with "happy thoughts" is a pedantic waste of time. Facing the pain head on is the surest route to happiness.

Pillar of Infinity

As measurement of the quantum-mechanical nature of reality has unfolded, there arises a principle known as the *Uncertainty Principle*. In general, this principle states that it is impossible to simultaneously measure both the *present position* and *future momentum* of a particle of energy.

The principle of uncertainty can be plainly observed with the physical eyes by observing the flames of a fire. While observing, hold the intention to simultaneously determine the position of a flame and its future momentum. In one moment of honest application of this exercise, it will be seen that it is impossible.

Attempting to logically deduce the flames current position and future momentum is an effort of foolishness. As it is, the future is yet to be determined. The present moment is the only actual point of determination in which all material and energy is currently radiating. From this basis is all potential possible.

Nothing outside of the potential contained in the present moment is possible, nor is it real. Only from the current moment is the future determined.

In terms of geometry, the point from which a ray originates fundamentally influences the succession of coordinates through which the ray flows. In other words, if a business man whose sole purpose is to make money for his own benefit, awakens from his slumber one night to see a new purpose, and consequently sells all his possessions and enters a monastery located in the hills of a remote mountain country for the sole purpose of focusing his whole mind, heart and soul on the alignment to source; then the nature of his journey fundamentally alters with that change of purpose.

Every individual is a field of energy with a unique mathematical set of variables. And within that field of uniqueness, the individual is directly situated in an all-encompassing field with infinite degrees of simultaneously present potential possibilities. No two individuals are exactly the same and no two individuals can live the exact same life. Every individual is a unique unit of infinity possessing infinite degrees of freedom pointing in infinite directions. And it is the spiritual heart (that which is meta-to-the-physical heart) that exists as an infinitude of primordial depth. And the nature of this infinitude is such that it is unyielding to its ever-present effulgent function – to love.

Consider each individual as a sphere, a complete unity in and of itself – whole. How many points of reference exist on the circumference of that sphere? An infinite amount; both to the outwardly infinite, and the internally infinitesimal.

Between two points there is always a middle point. The shortest distance between two points is a straight line, and in the middle of that journey from point A to point B is point (A + .5), or (B - .5).

The point of contemplation in all this is, that at the center of that sphere is the source-point of all possible points arriving at the circumference of the sphere, as a radiant expression of source-point energy. In other words, the center of the sphere is a singularity that is infinite in and of itself. This singularity reiterates extending its infinite nature outward through the sphere that is the individual of complete unity – wholeness.

An analogy of this is a set of Russian dolls, wherein a doll fits inside another doll that fits inside another doll; and at each level, it is the space inside the doll that gives it its functionality. Much the same, atoms compose molecules, molecules compose cells, cells compose tissues, tissues compose the human body, humans compose humanity, humanity composes only one spectrum of consciousness inhabiting this planet, and this planet composes only one planet of trillions in a universe that is infinite.

> The disciples said to Jesus, "Tell us how our end will be." Jesus said, "Have you discovered, then, the beginning that you look for the end? For where the beginning is, there will the end be. Blessed is he who will take his place in the beginning; he will know the end and will not experience death.
> Yeshua

Pillar of Unconditional Love

To look and *see* the innate perfection in everything, to emote and *feel* love for everything, to be and *radiate* source energy to everything; this is the *pillar* of unconditional love. The choice to recognize and consciously exist in this pillar is a choice to manage one's attention point with mental focus, emotional purity, and certainty of being.

A singularity of consciousness in the center of the heart spins and emits the radiation of source energy; thus, sourcing one's awareness. As this source energy moves through every aspect of one's being, it supplies life-force energy to the fields of awareness that give rise to the human form. The physical, mental, emotional, and spiritual bodies are dependent upon this singularity. Without it, the bodies, or fields of awareness would not exist.

In the geometric analogy of each individual being a sphere, with the center being a point of singular presence that supplies the individual with an infinite framework of operation; it is the individual's innate choice to extend that infinite framework to the rest of creation in full expressive radiation that bestows real freedom.

A definition of infinite is *without limit*. Another word to describe this quality of existence is *unconditional*. The unconditioned framework supplied to each individual from the singular source point is a framework that reiterates; meaning, the framework repeats itself over and over again in more expansive domains of functional symmetry.

For individuals conditioned by space and time, aligning one's point of perspective to the unconditional source acts a fundamental change in one's orientation to life. To orientate to the source of one's existence is to develop an inner harmony with that which is referred to by the term God. Only by faith is this journey possible for those who are blind to the spiritual universe. Faith is an extension of will – it is a choice to act in accordance with that which is unseen, and consequently unknowable through reason from a bottom-up perspective.

Although the spiritual universe is beyond physical sight, it is entirely within the reach of one's heart. For every unit of propagation, from the singularity that stand as the premise of one's existence, to the individual that exists as an interdependency of systems, to the whole of humanity, to the solar system, to the galaxy, to the universe and so on; the unconditional framework reiterates. The vector space complexifies. And the propagation of life rejuvenates itself in every moment that a sentient individual decides to consciously extend this unconditional framework.

God is Love.

A is A.

> For God so loved the world that he gave his one and only Son, that whoever believes in him shall not perish but have eternal life.
> Yeshua

And thus, the injunction is as follows:

> Therefore, focus your mind on Me, and let your intellect dwell upon Me alone through meditation and contemplation. Thereafter you shall certainly attain Me.
> Krishna

Who is God? God is Love. Fix the attention point of the mind on the centrality of Love and know this Singularity as the source and essence of all creation. This one injunction is the basis of all spiritual philosophy.

> Whatever is born, animate or inanimate, know them to be born from the union of Spirit and matter... The one who sees the same eternal Supreme Lord dwelling as Spirit equally within all mortal beings truly sees. When one beholds one and the same Lord existing equally in every being, one does not injure anybody; because one considers everything as one's own self. And thereupon attains the Supreme Abode... Anybody can attain the Supreme Abode by just surrendering unto My will with loving devotion
> Krishna

> 'Love the Lord your God with all your heart and with all your soul and with all your mind.' This is the first and greatest commandment. And the

second is like it: 'Love your neighbor as yourself.' All the Law and the Prophets hang on these two commandments.

Yeshua

Hence, the purpose of the Holy Life does not consist in acquiring alms, honor, or fame, nor in gaining morality, concentration, or the eye of knowledge. That unshakable deliverance of the heart: that, verily, is the object of the Holy Life, that is its essence, that is its goal.

And those, who formerly, in the past, were Holy and Enlightened Ones, those Blessed Ones also have pointed out to their disciples this self-same goal, as has been pointed out by me to my disciples. And those, who afterwards, in the future, will be Holy and Enlightened Ones, those Blessed Ones also will point out to their disciples this self-same goal, as has been pointed out by me to my disciples.

Siddhartha Gautama Buddha

Three Masters, arriving in different eras and cultures, all saying the same thing – A is A.

The child of God is the one who looks in the mirror and *sees* the One looking in the mirror. Salvation is through the relationship fostered by the individual and the Creator. The mind must first be fixed on the source of Love to extend that love to the rest of Love.

One must know one's *self* in order to fully function in the operation of the primary order. The mission is for those who elect themselves and volunteer for the ordination to the highest order.

Commitment of this degree is nothing short of complete and total abdication of all other values. One cannot serve two masters. One need not look outside oneself to arrive at the Master of all creation. The indwelling is an internal structure.

The label used to annotate the reality of what-*is* does not equate to the reality of it. The three-letter word that is God does not capture the totality of that which *is*. No word can.

> The kingdom of God does not come with your careful observation, nor will people say, 'Here it is,' or 'There it is,' because the kingdom of God is within you.
>
> Yeshua

Ever increasing awareness of the reality of God's nature as the causation of being is the most essential task of any self-aware individual. When the light of awareness strikes, choice is present. To willfully reject harmonizing with the source of being is a conscious denial of truth – sin. To extend the false notions of sin, is to extend illusion. And yet, in any moment of conscious awareness, an individual can choose to align to the Truth of all things. This willingness is fundamental in all steps towards the divine. Thus, it is a choice to become aware of the divine.

Chapter 2

Epistemological Axiom

To "know thyself" is the single most important function the mind can serve.

I Am Light

Knowledge – the active force of all action in the universe. Without it, no human choice is possible. With it, the wisdom of truth illuminates the mind. Openness is the necessary requisite of knowledge. The seed of knowledge will not grow in the infertile soil of resistance. Fertile soil is openness of being. To be intellectually receptive of the *eternal precepts of divinity*[4] is only the beginning. To be wholly receptive, mind, body and soul, is where real knowledge – Light – is seeded and grows. The power of real knowledge transcends the temporal and leads to the eternal.

Power, simply defined, is the ability to do work. *To do* implies action. In order to *do* something, one must be operating in a certain degree of a functional *knowing* of how to *do* it.

The axiomatic understanding of the metaphysical nature of an individual's reality is the *Be*; the *knowing* and the *doing* proceed forth from that source. Epistemology is the observance of *knowing*.

---

[4] This phrase, "eternal precepts of divinity" may hold no meaning for the reader, particularly if the reader's mind is subject to skepticism. If no meaning exists in the phrase for the reader, replace the phrase with "substratum acting as the foundation of the cosmological constant". If this new phrase also holds no meaning, it is recommended that the reader research the "cosmological constant", apply the denotations of the concepts contained in the phrase, and contemplate the phrase thoroughly.

According to the Army Field Manual No. 22-100, chapter 1 section 21:

> BE, KNOW, DO clearly and concisely state the characteristics of an Army leader... Leadership is about taking action, but there's more to being a leader than just what you do. Character and competence, the BE and the KNOW, underlie everything a leader does. So, becoming a leader involves developing all aspects of yourself. This includes adopting and living Army values. It means developing the attributes and learning the skills of an Army leader. Only by this self-development will you become a confident leader of character. Being an Army leader is not easy. There are no cookie-cutter solutions to leadership challenges, and there are no shortcuts to success. However, the tools are available to every leader. It is up to you to master and use them.

Knowledge is Power, i.e., *knowing*. This word is a verb that denotes a dynamic activity that *does* something. Thus, without knowledge, no *real* action is possible. With the application of the word "real" as used herein, it implies action that has an eternally sustaining effect. Actions of the order and sort that are impermanent with the nature of change are only real insofar as they are present in relative reality. Actions, or more specifically, decisions that have the absolute implications of eternity are more real in that the effects of those actions are perpetually sustained in the fabric of experience.

All things possess a certain degree of innate light. All things are operating at a basic level. The proof of this is the fact that a *thing* currently exists. All things, throughout the vastness of that which is real, are entirely dependent upon a stable source of informed energy – light. All constructs must necessarily be derived from a foundation that allows for the stability of continued existence. This stable foundation is the source and center of all information that is knowable, and consequently, actionable. The potential for a thing's existence is inherent in the stable source of informed energy that currently permeates all existence. The question is, what is actually knowable? Or rather, what is the expanse of real knowledge?

With this definition of knowledge, that only real knowledge actually exists in the absolute sense, it is assumed that knowledge creates effects of a sustained sort. It is also assumed that acting with illusion, or non-knowledge, creates effects that appear to exist momentarily, but are without lasting foundation. In the relative sense, knowledge of something can be concocted. In the absolute sense, that which is knowledge is forever true and always has foundation. One is as certain as this moment's perpetual existence; the other is as real as yesterday's magic show.

In the process of *knowing* herein defined, there are four motors that support the movement of the action; they are: 1) Overstanding, 2) Understanding, 3) Realization, and 4) Actualization. Each motor is a progressive expansion of the previous, culminating in revelation. Overstanding is a small unit of intuitional sensing that is connected to the source of all that is real. Understanding is an integrative function of rational comprehension based on experientially operating in tune with the overstanding. Understanding cannot occur without overstanding. Overstanding is innate and accessible at any moment; understanding is a progressive integration of overstanding.

Overstanding may be more accurately described as an orientation to one's *inner*-standing, and understanding may be more accurately described as an expression of the inner-standing. Openness is the function necessary to receive the information located at the point of view that is overstanding. Progressively, the clarity of one's prime directive is experienced and fully integrated, thus begetting realization, and with this a fundamental change in one's disposition to life occurs

– a change in character. And as one assumes the character expressed by the innate and supreme overstanding, actualization occurs with every *willful* action that is in tune with the reality expressed by the innate overstanding.

Currently, for the individual reading these words, if any degree of insight has been sparked by the match-light of these words, awareness has been sparked. That insight is the specific data that pertains to the individual soul construct of the reader. However, the awareness is only initiatory, a willingness to fully receive the input must be embraced; and this is a decision that pertains to the scope of responsibility inherent to the individual. Introspecting into the depths of the information available in the insight occurs through an openness of being. The development of this openness is the duty of the individual who sees the reality that these words point to. And again, willingness is required in the development.

An analogy to consider in processing the insight is that, overstanding is seeing the forest. Understanding is seeing the trees. Realization is seeing the forest and the trees simultaneously. And actualization is navigating through the forest by way of the map that has been constructed.

At any point in life, when insight into Truth arises, it is generally an initial overstanding. Seeing and feeling how the insight directly applies to the individual is seeing certain trees of the forest. Contemplation of the unchanging terrain features that land-mark the insight as a distinct insight helps to unfold the information contained in the data transaction.

In land-navigation, understanding terrain features and orientating a map, or mental perspective, to those terrain features is an active process of seeing the forest and the trees. Knowing one's specific location in the midst of a jungle based on observing the terrain is a high-level skill. The orientation of one's mental perspective begins the process of actively aligning one's being to the Truth contained in the insight.

To orientate the map is a skill requiring a mental capacity that supersedes fear and doubt. *Presence* is the tool required. In the still presence of one's mind is the rational capacity to arrive at a decision point in the context of the situation at hand – situational awareness. Fear constricts the body's receptiveness and is counter to the function of openness. Doubt closes the portals of the mind and does not allow insight to flow.

As it is, there is only one situation in life – the present one. All decisions proceed forward from this point of focus. The ability to choose necessarily derives itself from the rational mind. The primary function of the rational mind is choice.

In any given moment, the individual chooses what to focus the mind on, and in this, the rationality present in the mind is derived from that choice. Every individual is in a constant process of choosing thoughts. These thoughts are where one's attention point is located. Thoughts may initially occur at random, but every thought after the initial arrives through a subtle or distinct willingness to focus one's attention point in the direction of the thought.

In the analogy of navigating through the forest, an individual can be consumed by the thoughts and feelings that speak to being lost. Or, that individual can take a moment to breathe and presence self in situational awareness to assess the current position, the location of the sun, moon, or stars, the surrounding terrain features, the sounds of the forests, the fragrance of the air and the intuitional guidance present in the chest, stomach, and body.

Being consumed in the thoughts and fears of being lost is a darkness of non-knowledge. Presencing one's self to the moment brings stillness to the thoughts and fears associated with those thoughts, and allows for a rational clarity to bring the mind into a course of action.

Knowledge creates. What is real is true. What is not real is false. Fear is associated with the future. The future is not yet. The present moment always is.

Situational-awareness and Self-awareness are the epistemological roots of all knowledge. Knowing what is required in the moment and doing it is the solution to all situations.

Always increasing one's power through a universal-learning that occurs as an inner revealing is the method to stand in the fact of the epistemological axiom – I Am Light.

In every moment, an individual has the choice to become *aware* of self and life. When the willingness to embrace this choice is enacted, the axiomatic overstanding – I am light – is understood by direct experience.

Directly experiencing the reality of one's primary essence requires a rational orientation to the nature and scope of the vehicle through which the journey occurs, one's mind, body and soul. Mind necessarily derives it functional capacity from the basic constructs of the existing cosmic construct. The same is true with the soul. Each is primarily influenced by Spirit.

The Empire of Rational Knowledge

Rationality begets clarity. What is rational is that which is sane. Sanity can only be *enacted* when Reality is seen. Seeing illusion and enacting it is insanity. Insanity is not knowledge; it is the ignorance of knowledge.

To *be* rational in all thoughts and corresponding deeds, an individual must dis-integrate every thought stemming from illusion. Taking action with thoughts of illusion as the precursor to those actions begets more illusion. Moving in this domain of illusion is the state of confusion that is insanity – hell.

Rational knowledge is universal in its application, as it stems from that which is real. That which is real applies to everything because everything is founded in reality. That which is real is what gives rise to the present moment. The moment of Now is the only moment where *experience* is found. There is no other moment that can be experienced.

The activity of rational action can only occur in Reality. That which is not rational is based on an illusion that does not see Reality. Believing that the past creates this moment is insanity. Believing that a possible future circumstance can threaten this moment is insanity. Past events may have effects in this moment, but the past does not *create* this moment. And while a future circumstance may seem to have perceived effects that resonates with danger, the *stability* of the present continues regardless. The only domain of rational activity is in this moment where all Life vibrates in its universal essence.

Entering into this domain is entering into an Empire that has no limits on the ability to embrace the resonant reality that permeates the whole of existence. The only boundaries that apply towards entering this domain are the boundaries that an entity creates in the mind and makes-believe to appear as real. These boundaries are no more real than the national boundaries that separate one nation from another. These boundaries are a choice to have them *appear* as real, yet they are not. All it takes to dis-integrate these false boundaries is a choice to not believe in them.

To believe in an illusion is to place an idol on the altar of Truth and say it is real. The idol is a figment of the imagination and can never be real; it is only a figment and is not Truth. Only Truth is Truth. That which is not Truth is not real. To bring the mind into Truth is to dispel all illusion, and **this** is the entrance into the Empire of Rational Knowledge – a journey of facing revelation.

The journey does not shortcut the *fact* of subjective experience. Subjective experience may say one thing is true, but be entirely fostered by a long train of deceit. This also does not mean that subjective experiences are not real. An experience in the body is an experience in the body, which is factually true, as well as the thoughts and beliefs that allow the experience to remain in the body. What is true in a relative sense is not the same as Truth. Distorting these two concepts is where all confusion arises. Coming to see Truth as the highest value and being committed to living *that* Reality is where real freedom is. It is what the statement by Yeshua, "and the truth shall set you free," actually means.

In actuality, all individuals are already in the empire that is the Truth of Reality; it is merely a conscious re-cognition of it that allows it to be seen, integrated and fully experienced. Seeing clearly is the only way in which sanity can be enacted, and this is rationality.

The Empire within and without is the only domain where Reality can be seen. This domain is where Life arises into the expansion of Life. In the *living* is the giving nature of life, this is the Father principle of the Creator. All that is inheritable by a child is given by the Father. The Father gives his energy, the Mother receives it, and together a child is born with an innate potential to both give and receive. Due to the nature of the primal extension and reception, that which is not given is not real. That which cannot be given cannot be real, as it is not based in the reality that gives life to all existence. Deceit cannot be given, it is functionally without substance, and thus, anything stemming from deceit is wholly incapable of supporting life. Only Reality is functionally real, *assuming* otherwise is irrationality.

An individual's primal substance always lives because it is always being given by the prime Creator. Primal substance will never not be living. Beyond the perceptions of this moment and into the chamber (substratum) that allows this moment to *be* is the *living* (cosmological constant) that never fades. Engaging this chamber, and letting it infuse the entirety of the individual scope of existence, is the understanding that is the Empire of Rational Knowledge.

That which can be known can only be known with a mind that engages the fullest expanse that reality offers. Holding erroneous assumptions as an infallible and unquestioned truth leads to disease, whether mental, emotional, or physical. Disease cannot but lead to death. Death, as defined herein, is a perpetual denial in receiving the ultimate solution to life – Grace.

Objectivity

To see objectively is to see independent of the distortion of personal ambiguity. That which is objective fact is never wrong in the sense that it always accurately portrays the truth of the situation. To always see truth, a mind cannot accept falsity as a parameter. To function with the parameter of falsity or false reality, the output of such invalid input will consequently be irrational – garbage in, garbage out.

What is not real has no persistent meaning and as such has no real value. To believe in something of no value and invest personal attachment to that non-value creates the distortion of personal ambiguity. Personal attachment to non-value perpetuates a willingness that, in its functional scope, creates a space for the distortions of reality to occur, thus affecting one's experience. That which is unambiguous, in the sense that it is always certain, is that which always *is*.

Reality is always accurate, and that which exists, regardless of whether or not the individual thinks it exists, is the *overstanding* of the objective clarity of Truth. Beyond the personal identifications of what is thought to be real is the truth that actually *is* real.

What is perceived to be real is only a personal identification. Perceptions can never portray Reality *in its fullness*; they can only portray a fractional scope that arises from a situational experience. And although perceptions can lead to revelation, they are two distinctly different functions. Perception is an outward orientation; revelation is an inward expansion. Insofar as perception brings one to a fuller expression of inner truth, will the function of perception operate in its fullest capacity. The Light of Truth already *is*, and it need only be embraced. The *embracing* is fostered through a willingness to face revelation.

To look through the lens of "what's in it for me," and hold any personal attachment to the outcome of things based in that perspective is to remain in the uncertainty of personal ambiguity. The outcome of things holds no bearing on the fact of this moment. The things *of the world* are merely an effect of the underlying cosmic expression and do not dictate Truth, they extend it. The gift of this moment is such that reality exists; it is being given in an ever-sustained progressive movement.

Eternity implies an eternal past and an eternal future. Infinity implies eternity in all directions. These are the *gifts* of the Source of this moment's reality. This moment is not possible without a source-system that cannot encompass the scope of infinite eternity. By its very nature, the systemic source extends to an infinitely eternal past and into an infinitely eternal future, thus forever sustaining an ever-existing present moment.

That which is false is not real and cannot hold any actual meaning. To invest an identity in that which is not real is to personally identify with meaninglessness. Results are effects; to seek effects without taking into full consideration the cause is to perpetuate the illusion that claims separation from reality is the fundamental relationship to all things. Truth creates the possibility for all personal truths and thereby, all personal experience. Truth is always absolutely real while personal truths may only be relatively real.

Subjectivity

The only experience that an individual can experience is the experience that the individual experiences in the current moment. There is no other experience that an individual can experience; thus, the nature of an individual's experience dictates that an individual can only move into Truth and realize it only through a direct experience by that individual; this surmounts to Understanding.

Truth reigns beyond the subjective experience, and yet, Truth is wholly within the immediate reach of the individual. It is the subjective experience that is the only domain an individual has available to embrace the infinite scope of objective Truth. This is expressed in a statement of, "I only know what I know, I don't know what I don't know, and the only thing I can really know is what is given by this moment."

All Beings experience the same experience that is Experience. No Being experiences a different absolute reality and everyone experiences an entirely unique relative experience. The relative only pertains to the individual. The absolute is absolute in its perfection and all Beings exist simultaneously herein the absolute.

To perceive and believe that there is only a relative experience is to be lost in the confusion of insanity that attempts to subvert Now and construct something else in place of it. The perception of separation arises from this mental subversion. Experience of the absolute and the relative occur simultaneously. More specifically, relative experience arises from absolute experience. The individual relative experience is a derivative of the absolute. The absolute is the base from which all subjective entities are derived.

There is no possibility that Reality is not real, although it is true that relative realities are different. The specificity of the details inherent in the transient nature of the situation constitutes the subjective; and the absolute is the playground of all subjective relativities.

If two different absolute realities existed simultaneously next to one another, then separation would indeed be real. Yet, beyond the veil of the insanity that sees this split of "My God", "Your God" and

"No God" is the One Reality that can never be separated and contains all conceptions of "God".

It is the individual that must embrace the distinct specificity of personal experience. To deny this is to deny the opportunity to see Reality. Into the center of this experience is *that which* gives rise to all that is experienced. To deny this center is to deny the reality of one's actual Self that is created in the image and likeness of the Source. In this choice to deny Self is the choice to not love oneself, consequently not loving God or one's neighbors.

Remaining blind to Self is a factor of limitation. Self is that which is unconditional. Self must be directly experienced in the only domain where experience can be experienced. The only domain is now. This moment is the warehouse of all value. Remaining ever conscious in this moment moves the attention point into alignment with the transcendent Self that exists simultaneously everywhere and is also situated at the center of all things.

The gateway into freedom is through the moment in which all Life is housed. In the house of Life is the home that no Being has ever left. Since the beginning of all things, the Eternal House has always been ever-present. It is the willingness to knock on the door, which is fostered by the individual, which allows Life to respond. And Life does so by taking the door off the hinges. The Source of life is a parent that desires to give everything to its child; and when the child is open to receive that supreme gift, it will assist the child in all ways. The requisite is willingness.

Only the individual can make the choice to be willingly receptive of the grace that is always being given by the first cause of all that is. The first cause is the source and finality of every temporal and eternal construct, as every existing construct exists as an extension of the first cause.

The first cause is unknowable without directly and consciously experiencing the grace bestowed by that cause. That first cause is the primal and preceding effect of everything. It gifts this *cause-ability* to all who encompass the awareness of awareness. Choice is the function of the ability to be a cause, i.e., a root of causality. Being a cause that is in tune with the first cause is to exist in functional harmony with Life – to do the Will of God.

Unconditional Love

Light is replete and synonymous with Truth, as light is the actionable substance of Truth. Reason, the ability to think clearly, is the only justifiable avenue through which Truth is *enacted* in one's life. And if Truth is a repository of all real data, then light is that data moving, a transaction. And if data moving *is* the action present within existence, then the data of Truth moving through an individual gives the individual access to Truth.

All real information that is fundamentally knowable is composed of light. The data that currently moves through the body and gives it its existing structure is light. All things are composed of the data structure that is light. The light of awareness that operates in one's consciousness is the functional scope wherein an individual arrives at knowingness. Funneling this light through the mind and synergizing it with the amplifier that is the heart, brings an individual into a revelatory state-of-being wherein Knowledge can more fundamentally operate.

Knowledge, in the absolute sense of the word, holds a resonant degree of power that surpasses all constrictions of the world. This type of *knowing* is not a learned and habitual process. It is a knowing that acts in the space created by the willingness of the individual to be a receptive participant of the Life plan of the Creator. The space created is openness, and the life plan in its most basic function is to give life and liberty to all while pursuing one's own happiness. Orientating to this basic life pattern, each individual associates with the giving nature towards the unique proclivity inherent in the singularity situated at the center of one's being. And with that unique association, the giving of Life takes its many forms, shapes, colors, sounds, and vibrations.

To know one's Self is to know Reality; the realization of which walks across the bridge of knowledge and into the Reality of Truth – Unconditional Love. The truth of unconditional love is not a truth that can be logically understood without *application* of it. This empirical distinction approaches the ethical integration of this One Love. Unconditional love is a supreme abode of eternal wisdom that flows increasingly.

The constriction inherent to static conclusions based on self-assessed reality narrows the awareness of the entity trapped in positional awareness – narrow mindedness. To move beyond the perceptions clouded in the illusive reality of personal ambiguity involves moving beyond the identifications of a positional identity. From there, a blossoming of universal and spiritual identity can occur – an essential identity. If the perceived position is believed to be the total scope of self, the individual is limited to the personal identification that is "me", relative to that position.

The positional identity is merely a position through which unconditional awareness flows in and through, so as to experience a Self-relating feedback loop, such that the interaction is with its own unconditional awareness; this is the foundation of all relationships and why the first and most important injunction is to "love God, and love your neighbor as yourself".

The entity located at the position is neither the position, nor the perceived identification arising from that position. The entity is the structure of light that underlies that positional orientation; and is the unconditional awareness that flows through the position to interact with its own unconditional awareness.

> You are the Light of the World... let your light shine before others that they may see your good deeds and glorify your Father in heaven.
>
> Yeshua

For the entity with a mind trapped in the identifications of the position, the entity's identity appears to be the personal identifications arising from the position. Knowingness does not reach is total functional capability with this narrow-minded orientation. The *realization* of unconditional love occurs to release the mind of the entity trapped in positional identification. When the release of positional identity occurs, the mind and heart of the entity is then free to move in the fluidity and universality of unconditional awareness – I Am.

All knowledge within the reality of an entity's positional awareness, individuality, is subject to the empirical nature inherent within the process of understanding. The knowledge an entity operates with must be subjectively objectified with the direct experience of Truth; that is, Reality.

Direct experience of what is actually knowable is the only objective foundation through which an entity can truly understand anything. Understanding is the logical expression of a rational knowing and continued expression culminates in integration; it implies action. Knowledge is not truly understood until a distillation process synergizes the understanding with the innate and primal overstanding. From there the knowledge is expressed in the realm of experience. The full scope of this process is the path of Mastery.

As the positions of an energetic structure that is also a multi-dimensional reiterating singularity converge; the dynamics of the convergence between the relative points of reference compose the matrix of experiential reality. The singularity-point situated in each individual gives rise to the energy framework that exists as the soul structures of existing reality, such as the human form; and thus is the subjective nature of one's experience.

An *infinitesimal* singularity exists as a whole and *indivisibly* independent cause. This singularity simultaneously extends itself in all directions giving rise to reflective singularities that are made in the image and likeness – individuals. These reflective singularities also possess the inherent abilities of the original cause but are entirely dependent on the first cause to continue its extension. The extension of this basic energetic construct in its effects creates an existence that has variability in the manifolds of differential densities.

The total sum of these effects is wholly unknown because the effects continue to propagate in an ever-progressive cycle of involution and evolution. The present moment continues and change happens. Yet, at the base of all movement, the first and most primal movement is to extend or give. Thus, knowledge is not knowledge unless it is given.

The objectification process required to move in-tune with the ever-extending primal cause involves integrating the subjectivity of one's relative reality. Objectivity and subjectivity are merely aspects of the same conscious existence. The unification of the two is what takes an entity across a full spectrum bridge of all possible color frequencies; from the duality of separation and into the oneness of Unconditional Love.

A whole scope consideration of all elementary, primal and essential aspects of existence is brought to recognition through *living* life in the effulging[5] moment, and in this an entity remains liberated. Realizing the fundamental truth of now, an entity realizes the fundamental nature of the One unconditional reality that is Love – the life-giving source of existence – One Love.

---

[5] The movements of the existing essence of all reality in the process of becoming all that is concurrently throughout all of the present existing reality.

Freedom exists now, not in some idea of the future or any philosophical construct. The reality of Unconditional Love is realized in the freedom existing now. If the desire is for freedom, what rational reason could there be to delay the process of revelation?

Chapter 3

Ethical Axiom

No choice is present to not exist in the current moment. Only from this instant does all action proceed forth.

I Am Integrity

The metaphysical approach orients one's *being,* the epistemological approach orients one's *knowing,* and the ethical approach orients one's *doing*. In an overly simplistic sense, an individual has two choices for doing; to do good or to do evil. Either option proceeds forth from the orientation of one's being and knowing.

Illusion is a factor wrought out by a functioning consciousness that denies the insight of Truth. Evil is the product of illusion. Evil does not actually exist; there is no substance to it. Evil can only affect an individual who has not fully surrendered to the impenetrable certainty of Truth. Good is all that is. To assume that the source of all reality creates ill-will assumes that the source breeds hate. Hate denies life, love extends it.

In a reality where free-will is innate to sentient beings, the potential to not operate in tune with the prime directive is inherent. The potential must exist if a creature of will is to truly have the freedom to choose to be a willing participant *with* life. It is not that the source creates evil, it is that the source has created beings with immense power to create and the freedom to choose any direction of their pleasing. In this absolute law of cause and effect, the individual is the cause; whereas the effects of evil are due to the ignorant operation of one's consciousness.

Evil is only evil because it acts contrary to the Prime Directive. This is only true because it is this directive that supplies the framework for reality to exist. The only thing that can be functionally real is that which stems from the fundamental basis of all reality. A framework that attempts to circumvent the basis cannot be functionally real, thereby establishing its "evilness".

Individuals operating in ignorance are the cause of evil, yet, evil is wholly without absolute substance. The effects of evil are bound to time and the effects of time are undone when the individual binds one's soul to everlasting Truth – the Prime Directive.

The clarity of this injunction, which is to be a cause in tune with the first cause, operates by way of the function of honesty. Honesty bestows to the individual a degree of freedom that transcends any and all effects of the world.

Confusion is inherent in illusion. Illusion extends false conceptions of reality. Adopting a mental paradigm that has false conceptions at its base is to adopt a perspective of ignorance. Ignorance, in its effect, is a turning away from real knowledge; consequently, turning away from reality.

The vehicle to clarity is honesty. Using an inner orientation to honesty as the standard for thought, word and deed is a purification process that uproots all forms of irrationality. At first, this orientation may seem like grasping a rose by its thorns, and for an individual who is unskilled with honesty, this may be the experience. But it does not have to be so.

The skillful use of honesty is a soothing and sweet nectar that removes the thought-forms laden with toxic emotions. Honesty is firstly, an inner orientation to always seek the truth in all situations; and secondly, it is a distillation process that brings one to the freedom of transparency.

To hide something is to be constrictive with oneself, the consequence of which is to *not love*. To constrict is to close. To hide is to constrict. To be deceitful is to hide. What is the purpose of fabricating a false reality if a false reality only breeds the toxicity of confusion?

Fear is the motive of deceit. Yet fear is an imperfection. The value of fear is that it is a signal that Love can be activated. Doubt of the efficacy of love is only another form of fear. Fear persists insofar as the individual chooses to not trust life. Faith in the unseen supersedes fear of the seen insofar as the individual is willing to have the courage to trust in the power of love.

Honesty, in conjunction with an openness to Truth, fostered by a willingness to surrender to it, initiated by the divine leadings of the essential self is a way to the transparent expression of Self – Freedom.

> That unshakable deliverance of the heart: that, verily, is the object of the Holy Life, that is its essence, that is its goal.
>
> Buddha

Two Methods of Experience

> There is neither Self-knowledge, nor Self-perception to those who are not united with the Supreme. Without Self-perception there is no peace, and without peace there can be no happiness. Because the mind, when controlled by the roving senses, steals away the intellect as a storm takes away a boat on the sea from its destination – the spiritual shore of peace and happiness.
>
> Krishna

Wherein does one orient to the perspective of Self? Experience in its fullest spectrum is summed up in the word Harmony. Experience in its splintered and chaotic disorientation is summed up in the word Disharmony. There is only one true perspective on life. The degree to which an individual opens up to the immutable Truth of all things is the degree to which the individual tunes into the prime directive of the source and center of all things.

There are really only two modes to exist, one is to harmonize with that prime directive, and the other is to deny it. The habitual and unconscious denunciation of Truth is ignorance. The conscious and deliberate denunciation is evil. Whether through ignorance or evil, if an individual denies the knowledge-fruit offered from the Tree of Life, that individual resonates in a disharmonic state of being wherein suffering plagues one's experience. And yet, at any moment, the individual has the choice to slow down, sink into presence, move towards openness and receive the soothing waters of the spiritual Self.

In every situation, the prime directive of the Creator is operating in the depths of the individual's essential S elf. It is the foundation of oneself. Orientating to this perspective is the act of harmonizing to life. The act is a conscious, deliberate, and willful attempt to seek and reveal the Truth. To come into a personal and intimate relationship with the Creator. This one task is the most essential and primal task all individuals may embark upon – Facing Revelation. All other journeys eventually lead to this one. All paths lead home, and home is always a choice away.

Dying in Dishonesty

Rejecting truth is dishonesty. There is no small lie. Every rejection of the facts of reality is a subversion of the clarity of the mind. There is no rational thought in dishonesty.

The disease of irrationality acts as a fog covering the mind's luminous capacity. The density of the fog is inversely determined by the willingness fostered by the individual. The more an individual holds to beliefs without validating the truth of it by direct experience, the thicker the fog. The more willingness an individual cultivates so as to subject the mind to Truth by directly experiencing the knowledge fruit, the less dense the fog.

Thought is an active process and all action in the universe emanates from this primal cause. Beliefs cause thoughts and thoughts cause movement of the physical universe. The entire universe is a thought-function of the Creator. The Bible states, "In the beginning was the word and the word was with God, and the word was God." What is the knowledge that expresses as "the word" that is "God"?

Dishonesty, in its demonstration, is the action of speaking a word to hide a thought-function. Hiding one's *self* from oneself denies one's self the opportunity to know thyself – freedom. The denial of freedom is death. Suffering is the consequence of dishonesty. Hell is the state of suffering and death is its mode of existing. Eternal death is the result of dishonesty and eternity is always Now.

All aspects of experience that induce suffering shed light on the **opportunity** to cultivate a willingness to turn toward Truth. Suffering is a signal to be more honest with oneself.

> If you hold to my teaching, you are really my disciples. Then you will know the truth, and the truth will set you free.
>
> Yeshua

Living with Integrity

Integrity acts as a force of unification bringing together aspects of one's self-awareness through a unified expression of essential energy. Awareness is the initial step. The movement from unconscious thought patterns to conscious decisions is done so inside the vehicle of awareness. Making the decision to harmonize with unconditional love extends willingness forth from one's energy field, from which a space opens for honest introspection into the transparency of Spirit. **The choice of harmony is always in the present moment.**

Resolving all internal conflict and bringing the mind to unshakable tranquility cultivates an interior space to hold one's attention point on the heart – the throne of God. This is Self-Perception.

Self-Perception is neither egotistic nor arrogant. To perceive the true Self that exists as an extension and child of the Creator is to undo all self-deprecating tendencies, while humbling oneself with the awe induced by recognizing the Creator residing as the centrality of beingness. As this process unfolds inside the individual, revelation is taking place. The brightness of the lightning-flashes of Truth is enough to render the individual blind to the total scope of the Truth revealed. Each flash of Truth requires time to integrate, which presents itself as decisions to be made. And each flash brings the individual into more intimate contact with the Creator so long as the Truth is consciously integrated into a way of being – "to do the Father's will."

The will of the Creator is the prime directive that sustains the whole of existence and provides all nourishment in all its forms. To be a gifting agent or extension of this Will is to increase the capacity to receive this gift from the Creator. In order to give, one must first be willing to receive, this requires openness. From there, the gifting acts through every honest act of willful extension of love and service. Selfless service is the science of a sacred art that engages this degree of integrity. The sacredness of this art lies in the willful emulation of the supreme Will.

Integrity implies a certain degree of integration with a standard of conduct. Integration with the standard of unconditional love circumvents egoic distortions. The science of selfless service involves a mental focus that, in its effect, disengages the ideas and thought-constructs that has the individual seek towards opportunities that only benefit self. In selfless service, the injunction is to uplift all, including oneself. Who can uplift all but the one whose feet are securely planted on a secure foundation? What foundation is more secure than that which gives rise to the very existence of all things?

Chapter 4

Aesthetical Axiom

> That which proceeds forth from this moment
> is neither separate nor independent from existence.

I Am Life

The blood of the spiritual body is an energy force that permeates all space and exists as the foundation for time and space – made in the image likeness. The energy force exists as the primordial potential from which all manifested forms derive their sustenance for existing in continued effulgent emergence. Neither can this energy be seen directly, nor can it be separate from any object existing in space-time reality.

Focusing the mind into the heart and connecting the circuitry of energy, a vehicle of expression is created. This vehicle transports the individual to a domain of life propagating itself in every possible direction. This shift of consciousness is entering fully into life in which a conscious merger occurs – I Am Life.

The chariot wherein life propagates outward in an infinite number of directions, from the center point of the heart, is a vehicle of spiritual fire that knows only the transparency of eternal effulgence – The Kingdom of God is in the Heart.

> Whatever is born, animate or inanimate, know them to be born from the union of Spirit and matter... The one who sees the same eternal Supreme Lord dwelling as Spirit equally within all mortal beings truly sees. When one beholds one and the same Lord existing equally in every being, one does not injure anybody; because one considers

everything as one's own self. And thereupon attains the Supreme Abode.

Krishna

The World as a Mirror

Everything an individual perceives is a mere reflection of that which lies within one's being; reflecting the inner feelings and thoughts, either unconsciously or consciously. The world is the greatest mirror showing to the individual what must be embraced with forgiveness. In all occasions of judgment and condemnation of others, the individual is offered an innate look into the fallacy of one's own thinking. Judgment of others is an internal function of thought that does not encompass the total scope of the one being judged. In the act of judging, the one who *declares* the rigid and conclusive premise in attempt to encapsulate another in a certain and specific understanding, is the one who is emphasizing the ignorance resting *in one's own mind*.

The projection of the externally perceived world in the mind of the perceiver filters through a matrix of beliefs before it is made manifest as an "understanding" of the world. To seek the Truth in the world requires a merger with Truth in one's own self. Truth in the world can only be recognized when Truth in one's own self is recognized. How can one seeking to be saved know where salvation exists except if there is an inner recognition of that salvation that resonates with anything external? To foster the merger with Truth, the more an individual is willing to question every assumption, the more space the merger process has to take place.

All *things* in the world of form arise from the world of spirit. In all interactions of *things* is the interaction of the spirit in the purest expression of Reality. Every interaction with a space-time construct is an opportunity to merge with Truth.

As the world *appears* through perception it is merely the world of form, yet, beyond that veil of perception is the Reality that is vibrating now. The transparency of reality becomes ever-more apparent after an individual enacts honest introspection into the standard of all value. The standard permeates all existence and is a spiritually essential reality. Clarifying the concept of "spiritual", or any similar concept, is a distinct phase of the journey of honest introspection.

Perceptions, as they are sensed by the perceiver, can only arise in the mind of the perceiver. Those perceptions are merely playing out what the perceiver chooses to light with awareness. The view of perceived life is a direct reflection of that which the perceiver thinks and feels. Those who see imperfection see it because they fail to embrace the perfection of Now.

There is nothing that is not created sinless this moment. Grace is a gift from the source of this moment. Proof lays in the choice to reconcile, or not. Everything is reborn in the divine perfection of every existing moment. Forgiveness is the process whereby perfection is realized by the individual. Repentance and Forgiveness exist on the same coin, where one is, the other is also. That coin is called Reconciliation.

The only separation from realizing the divine in every moment are the internal agreements to not see or hear the divine. The mental *narrative* that perpetuates those internal agreements can be re-written in any moment – this is where free-will is found. Choice is at hand.

The key to understanding the past is to put it in its proper context – the past. It is no longer experientially real. There are, however, residual energy patterns that remain. Reconciliation is the process of flushing out those stagnant energy patterns.

If an individual does not want to feel the suffering that is associated with the memory any longer, the emotional resonance can be released with forgiveness. In fact, in those moments of reliving the energy patterns of the past, it becomes a perfect opportunity to dive into the suffering and dissolve the energy pattern. These opportune moments are prime situations to organize an energy pattern that resonates in a tonal frequency of purity; thus, moving ever more into the stream of life.

In the moments of *negative reflection*, wherein the mind dwells on the past, the judgments and conclusions that are drawn only serve to put up an invisible wall in the matrix of the mind. These negative reflections create a deeper split between the perceived self and the Self of that which *is* – I Am.

All the unresolved issues that an individual has with the past will surely seep into everyday thoughts about the world and people, consequently projecting a similar future. In that process, what an individual fails to resolve will reflect itself in the world – inner conflict begets world conflict. Inversely, inner peace begets world peace.

Releasing the mind from the clutches of the past, and living according to the Value of that which is Self, an individual sees the true nature of everything. When walking this journey of reconciliation, facing everything an individual must face, reveals an inner sanctum that is inviolate – the Sacred Heart.

With the freedom of Unconditional Love, there are two most basic choices; reflection or deflection. This can also be seen as harmony (reflection) or disharmony (deflection). It is an action of *acceptance* or *ignorance*.

Value Deflection

Deflection, in this context, is a conscious or unconscious choice to avoid facing reality. *Value* deflection is a way of *being* where invisible walls of conclusions create a philosophical point of view, wherein duality dominates the idea of reality.

From the initial avoidance, a natural chain of avoidances takes place. Eventually, this tendency to avoid leads to an unbalanced state in the energy fields of the individual. From this unbalanced state, an individual is inclined to seek validation elsewhere. Persistent validity is not attainable on an impermanent foundation. That which is impermanent must be seen for what it is. Seeing impermanency is the beginning of the journey to face revelation. According to the premises outlined herein, any attempt to find persistent validity in anything other than supreme love is disharmonic to the natural state of existence. Thus, value deflection is nothing more than disharmony. The key to the distinction being communicated is found in the understanding of Value as an abstract concept.

Generally speaking, the concept of "Value" acts as a pointer to something. What it points to is generally the specific instance of a particular *thing* that holds a certain degree of meaning for an individual. From this context, *value deflection* occurs when an individual moves about in life from the perspective of "win-lose".

Value as an abstract concept establishes the premise that all individuals have different specific instances of values. Yet, the unseen basis of the *valuing* act arises from the same place regardless of the individual and the specific *value* instance. A sense of this "unseen basis" can only be sensed as a somatic experience. The attempt to deny individuals, including oneself, the opportunity to freely *value* life in all its various forms is an act of value deflection – coercion.

The more inclined an individual is towards denial, the less the individual is open to the restorative experience of the *valuing* process. The output of such a disposition tends towards irrational pessimism; the proclivity to always seeing what's wrong with a situation and do little to turn the situation around. Individuals experiencing an addiction of any form implicitly understands the function of denial. These individuals may not consciously grasp the context of the situation, but they do experientially grasp the effects that stem from denial, i.e., value deflection.

At the basis of value deflection is a fundamental misalignment with reality – disharmony. The lack of agreement, disharmony, with reality can only be turned around by an internal shift in disposition by the individual. This internal shift is the idea of "I Rise".

Parsing out the idea of freedom, and focusing solely on the notion of free-will in the context of making a decision to shift the disposition of one's internal relationship to life is the functional scope of the algorithm extrapolated herein.

Value Reflection

Far from an ideological fluff cloud, harmony with reality is the only basis from which integrated happiness can arise. Reflection, in its mental function, engages a spectrum of abilities that transcend into the deepest of frameworks. At its maximal functional capacity, reflection is seeing the true essence of everything, not necessarily with the physical eyes but with one's entire *being*. Value reflection in its fullest functional scope is *embracing* the true characteristics of Life. In every moment, Life is present. If it wasn't, there would be no existence. Unconditional Love is ever present. Opening to this Love is what allows it to be seen, felt, and consequently experienced.

Reflection is a contemplative process and is as limitless as the imagination. The conscious use and deliberate direction of this function is tantamount to being the cause of one's experience. As it is, every individual who has come into the full maturity of the human brain has every freedom to dwell in misery or uplift in hope, to squander in suffering or elevate in faith, and to perpetuate violation or extend love.

The key that unlocks the door of true freedom is experiencing *that* love simultaneously with the body, mind and soul. One of the most effective means to be aware of it is by giving it in a *whole-hearted* and transparent expression – forgiveness. When an individual gives Love in a free expression of the heart, there is no other option but to see the love everywhere and be caught up in the rapture of it. When this takes place, all stress and concerns melt with the awesome power of the *revelation* involved in this process. The revealing, the blossoming, the unfolding. This does not mean that prudent planning and proper organization for future endeavors is not useful, it simply means the Spirit of unconditional love becomes the guide and pinnacle of those endeavors.

Love is everything. It manifests itself as an unconditional force giving itself to everything. To see it as something other than an unconditionally loving force is attempting to subvert its natural order; it goes against existence itself.

The goal is to arrive at a place within oneself that sees this value in everything. As Buddha stated it, "that unshakable deliverance of the heart". When this happens, the reflection of true existence is seen. It is of no concern when or where this happens, the location is irrelevant. It can be experienced everywhere. It is everywhere and exists as everything. Reflection is how an individual experiences one's *self*. Whether the experience is of suffering (deflection) or of joy (reflection) depends on where the individual places the attention point of the mind – it's a choice.

When the mental function of reflection occurs, and is directed through the portals of one's being into the depths of eternity, the process takes on a transformative effect. Nothing that touches real love will remain the same. All things are forever altered by the supreme goodness of love's everlasting nourishment.

Although love is everywhere, it is the awareness of love's consciousness inherent in an individual's heart that allows it to be Seen and Heard. Its revelation revolves around the free-will choice to embrace it. Without the choice to embrace love, there is no possibility the love will be unreservedly accepted, and thus, fully experienced.

If an individual seeks to bring about world peace, the conscious choice to *see* and *feel* the unconquerable peace within one's heart must be made. That Being must first be able to see it within and from that place, it naturally flows out and is made manifest in the physical through the direct action of that radiant energy.

When this pouring out of love occurs, an individual is then able to see it everywhere and hear it everywhere, in effect, holding the space for it. That individual would then be referred to as one "who has eyes to See and ears to Hear". The discerning truth of love is ever guiding the conscious awareness of that individual's operational choices.

This degree of perception is not limited to the physical sense of seeing and hearing. It is the sense that deals with the awareness of radiating fields of spiritual consciousness, expanding and enveloping real space and existing in present-moment time. From this awareness, all truth is revealed when the conscious *movement* is aligned with the truth that is embraced.

The only action that must take place is to embrace the centrality of that which is I Am. This choice revolves around *willingness*. Willingness extending forth as intention. True *will* arises from Unconditional Love. There are no conditions on the love that is given. It gives because it gives, and in giving it receives. In receiving, it has the ability to give more, and in giving more it has the ability to receive more *ad infinitum*.

All knowledge, truth, wisdom, understanding and consequential realization comes from this initial reflection of the natural order of Unconditional Love. The initial reflection is the willingness to openly receive it, and then give unconditionally to all existence existing in unconditional love *as* unconditional love.

To act from a place not aligned with the openness of the unconditional love is to act from a place that is opposed to the very essence of Life. Acting from this place of constriction, a natural chain of deflections occur that seems as though existence is separated and limited.

Acting from the truth of love, a natural reflection of the beauty of Unconditional Love arises to elevate the individual to a place of sublime perfection. Acting with unconditional love naturally reflects the beauty of unconditional love in each and every moment. What could be more reflective of beauty than that which gives rise to all beauty?

Chapter 5

Political Axiom

Wherever there is an interaction of existing constructs, politics is present.

I Am Creator

Existing *as everything* is the source *of* all things. From the centrality of *this* singularity's effulgence that is ever-persistently permeating all space and time; the congruence of interaction is such that all matter is an extension of this singularity.

A personhood that has been extended forth in ubiquity from the central singularity is endowed with creative free-will – *made in the image and likeness*. Choice is ever present for the individual who becomes aware of this premise.

When two personalities come into interaction, there exists two fields of sentience such that they are present to a multitude of choices. When the creative potential of two or more individuals becomes active in the individuals, the potentiality increases by orders-of-magnitude greater than any one individual's potential – synergy. And it is by the choice of each individual to enter into synergistic relationship *toward* an output of much greater significance.

> For where two or three come together in my name, there am I with them.
> — Yeshua

Bridging one's character into the pristine quality of the central source and interacting with all life from that place, brings to light a political atmosphere of integrity and honesty. In this atmosphere of transparency, an environment of harmonic synergy is established.

With an illuminated atmosphere of interaction among all constituents, a civilization of informed citizens can then consensually interact to engage creation in a fuller capacity.

World of Fear

Isolation in confusion, this is the nature of fear. Distrust, uncertainty, and doubt, these are the modes of transmission in the world of fear. In all ways that an individual senses separateness and disconnectedness, that individual's attention point has ventured into the dark forest of fear.

Fear, as it pertains to the human mind, is necessarily derived from its sense of primal self-preservation. To keep the body alive is a basic injunction, and fear is a powerful motivation toward that end. Given a situation where it is to kill or be killed, the body instinct is to kill. But why?

The unknown of the death process suggests that there is no valid way to determine what lies beyond. For a mind ensnared by boundaries of time, death seems to be a finality of personality survival. A primal fear arises from this dilemma.

Deep anxiety about the unknown is fear. So deep that it necessarily clouds the way an individual sees self and the world in any given context. Succumbing to fear and being consumed by its death grip colors one's experience towards self-preservation *by any means necessary*. The nature of this death grip works itself out in many subtle nuances of the body's emotional variations. At the root of it all is a mental uncertainty.

Fear is always related to a projection of the future, and the future is a construct of time. What is time to the present moment? And what is space to a construct that has yet to come into being? If space is simultaneously everywhere, and time is a measurement of that space's existence, then what does the future hold that can threaten the cosmologically constant space-reality?

If fear is related to an un-manifested or future construction, such as the death of personal existence, or the suffering related thereto, then fear is always a *current* experience related to a *time* construct.

In terms of fear and death, what is a father to do if a murderer is threatening the well-being of his family? Does he run and hide? Does he become angry and exact revenge? Or does he become present to the moment and move in the natural rhythmic flow to subdue the murderer and preserve his family?

What about the nation who is threatened by terrorists domestically and abroad? Does the national administration go on a man hunt for any perceived threat of national security both internal and external? Does the administration raise the white flag and surrender to the behests of the terrorists? Or does the administration promote international integrity by fostering the well-being of all people by acts of service toward uplifting those who wish to receive it in mutually beneficial ways?

In these situations, which is the way of fear? And which is the way of love? Decisions are ever persistent. Action only comes after a decision has been made. There is no action unless there is decision. The body does not move unless by decision. In moments of fear, with a mind that can be actively tuned into situational awareness, moving *with* the motivations of fear is cowardice and is a perpetuation of terror in one's personal experience.

Fear will never know the wisdom required to navigate relationships with honor. Honor of self and others will never be fostered by succumbing to fear. In that, the elevation of humanity will never occur through the subjugation, coercion, and persecution of others.

Social unity will only arise out of a space of political collaboration based on consent. The freedom to choose to collaborate politically is a given. Coercing an individual to collaborate is *not* collaboration.

Moving with the motive of fear in any way, necessarily short circuits the peace inherent in the heart of the individual. That which extends peace to the heart, also extends the guidance necessary to live in a world where relationships are ever-present. This guidance is not a matter of becoming an un-thinking zombie to an ideological myth of peace. The guidance urges the individual to think out solutions to problems, in all their complexities, with peace as the highest value.

The guidance will offer suggestions, open doorways, and make possible certain opportunities, but it remains always in the rational working-out of the individual's intellect – the moral necessity to choose to act with that guidance. The guidance will never make the decision for the individual; it will only offer its assistance. Fear, however, will cover over this whole process in the same instant an individual gives way to its dominance in the experiential domain.

Fear is the dark cloud of subversion that moves to undermine the moral footing of the individual. The logical conclusion in the morality of fear necessarily looks at situations from a self-infatuated point of view. Moreover, being consumed by fear does not allow for the possibility to extend a point of view to see the situation from the opposing forces. Existing in the stalemate of this quandary is the summation of a cold war.

Fear neither solves problems nor creates opportunities; it merely perpetuates existing dilemmas in varying complexities. And although fear is an elixir of degradation, it is *the choice to be consumed by it* that is the most devastating.

Fear reacts; this is the extent of its consciousness. It does not allow for full rational thought, nor does it allow for contemplation of solutions. The disposition of certain situations may seem such that there is no time for rational thought or contemplation. And that current and immediate action must be taken. In such circumstances, the movement with fear may alleviate the impending threat, but not necessarily so.

What offers more wisdom toward the effective navigation of such circumstances; blind reaction based in an energy dominated by self-preservation, or conscious presence in a domain where all creativity exists? What shall one do, when confronted with evil, perpetuate the underlying nature of evil, or extend goodness?

World of Love

Offering Value is offering love. This value is either given, exchanged, or held. Each movement is a choice made by the individual. Love has many forms. The form with which to offer love is dependent on circumstance, save the form of unconditional love.

Unconditional love begins to take noticeable effect when the individual resolves to engage forgiveness of self, and forgiveness of others. In the ability to relate with **all others** does the label "unconditional" begin to show its meaning. *The state of mind that views reality from an unconditional perspective accepts the freedom of others as a basic and intrinsic quality.* This state of mind also sees the reality of the Law of Cause and Effect.

For every decision that initiates action, an effect is certain to come about. The effect is of like-nature to the decision and is a perpetuation thereof – karma. The nature of the decision is predisposed to the state of mind that originated it. To solve a problem, the perspective must be raised to a higher elevation in order to gain a fuller perspective of the situation.

The elevation/illumination of consciousness occurs through forgiveness. Only when a mind is able to relax its point of view, such that it considers a perspective it has not seen, can it then begin to see beyond the narrow confines of an isolated individuality.

All forms of love other than unconditional are conditioned. Conditioned to the scope of the form and reasoning justifying the form. The form is dependent upon the context of any given situation. The form of love from husband to wife is different than love from parent to child. And yet, there is unconditional love as the deeper root to each instance of conditional love.

Which is more powerful for a child to hear; "I love you because you exist, I always will, and nothing will ever change that," or, "I love you because you get straight As in school." Which is unconditional, and which is conditional?

A child who is valued for sole the reason that the child exists, is a child who exists in a different environment than one who is valued only for what that child produces.

The underlying dynamic demonstrated in the example above is present in all relationships. Every relationship is founded in a Being of sentience interacting with another. Even the relationship of an individual to non-sentient life. By way of the interaction happening between two objects of space reality, relationship is present.

Who shall be the one to enact the injunctive disposition of spiritual character, except the one who wisely chooses to be in tune with the Premise from which spiritual character arises?

Bridges out of the World of Fear

1.

Have you ever looked in the mirror and wondered who that person staring back at you really is?

The image, floating on the surface of that mirror, staring right back at you, and you have no idea who it really is.

Lost in a haze of confusion, you look at your life, and you know you've done wrong.

You look at all the sins, all the things that make you guilty for the atrocities you have condemned upon yourself and others.

In that moment, your mind splinters with anxiety, and in the pit of your stomach a dark ball of suffering is eating you from the inside out.

Stinging pierces your neck as you begin to gag on the saliva in your throat. Fear is sucking your breath away as you begin to gasp for air while you watch your world fall in on itself. Everything you have ever dreamed of tumbles down while depression zaps you with a surge of death – welcome to Hell.

Look into the eyes of that image in the mirror, and ask it, "Who are you?" (Be warned: do not get trapped in self-deprecating idolatry).

2.

Are you a quiet person with your anger?

Anger is an emotion of the human animal, as is fear, but what do you do with that energy?

Swallow it and let it build?

Be controlled by it and let it out?

Or transmute it and *be free*?

What is Your *process*?

3.

"Hang on," said the old man with a crooked posture and no upper teeth, to the young man who stood leaning against the porch. "Yous in fo a treat." The old man limped through the door of the dilapidated cabin. "Come on in," he grumbled.

"Yes-zur," Charlie kindly replied.

Charlie followed the old man into his cabin, shut the door, and continued following him. The old man slowly sank into a rocking chair of small tree branches.

"Grab a seat Charleh," the old man drawled, "n brin me at glass on tha table oer yawnder."

Charlie reached down, grabbed the mug on the table, "This one?"

"Eh," the old man grunted as he nodded his head yes.

Charlie looked down at the mug in his hand and noticed two pyramids in gold paint, bottom to bottom in the shape of a star octahedron, as glitter-paint stars glistened in the background. *What the hell is that,* Charlie thought to himself.

"That my son is definitely not hell," the old man spoke with a deep, slow, and annunciated voice. "That is your chariot of fire blazing with Divine Light. It is the reason you are here, the Life vessel of your essence."

Charlie blinked slowly noticing that the old man's posture suddenly took on an aura of dignity, said nothing, and stared back at the old man while handing him the mug.

"Please sit if you so desire," the old man pointed to the chair on the other side of the rust-colored cast-iron stove. "Would you like some green tea, Charlie?"

"No thank you," Charlie replied as he sat in the chair while continuing to look at the old man with earnest curiosity.

"Why do you stare at me so, Charlie?"

"Uh, well, you just read my mind."

The old man shifted his eyes upward, "I suppose it could be stated as such." He looked at Charlie, "May I ask you a question?"

"Yeah, sure," Charlie said.

"Why is it that you are surprised I read your mind?"

Charlie looked down, then back up at the old man "Well, I guess I never really knew it was even possible."

"And that is reason to be surprised?"

"Yeah, why wouldn't it be?"

"There is much you do not believe to be possible, or could imagine as possible for that matter. If you are astonished by its mere possibility, your mind has yet to be free?"

"What do you mean my mind has yet to be free?" Charlie quickly replied.

"Do you really want to go down that rabbit hole Charlie?"

"What rabbit hole?"

"The rabbit hole you are looking at with curiosity?"

Charlie looked at the old man, his throat beginning to tighten and his chest burn. "WHAT fuckin rabbit hole!"

"The rabbit hole you are now in." The old man smiled softly.

Charlie shook his head and chuckled, *I can't believe this guy*, he thought.

"Why can you not believe me Charlie?"

"Would you stop doing that!"

"Stop doing what?"

"Reading my mind."

"Charlie," the old man softly said. "You are projecting it out there for all to see, if you do not want me to see it, leave it as an unformed thought in your mind, or let it go altogether. I am only guilty of being honest with myself; it is where the clarity to *see* comes from."

"You mean, you see my thoughts, my actual thought just because I think them?"

"All is plain to see through the Eye of honesty, Charlie. It all depends on how honest *you* allow yourself to be."

His foot began tapping as he noticed himself tensing his hands into fists. Charlie leaned his head back. Then looked at the old man. He sat there for a moment sensing the heat boiling through his chest and arms. *Fuck, I'm angry*, he thought. He sat up straight, glanced down to the floor and back again at the old man. "What the hell are you talking about old man?"

The old man stared back at Charlie, saying nothing. Quietly the two stared at each other. The old man was silent, composed with a peaceful vibe emanating from his presence. Charlie stared back with a quiet glare.

A smile emerged on the old man's face and quickly morphed into a heinous grin.

The old man's eyes glazed over with a deep stare, his pupils dilated wide, then flashed back to normal an instant later. Charlie seized backwards as a hammer plummeted from his throat to his stomach, crushing the righteousness he had established with anger. His knees became unable to hold still, the fear had spoken, and Charlie wanted to run.

"You see me Charlie," the old man said, "but you know not who I am."

"Who are you then," he quickly squeaked out.

"I see you still want to walk down that rabbit hole," the old man said. "You are a curious one Charlie, someday, that curiosity may kill you. That is of course if you don't free yourself with it first."

Charlie looked at the old man for a moment. "Old man, I think I better be going."

"I know Charlie, and if that is what you choose, then that is what you choose. Consider this before you go however." He paused, waiting for Charlie to look him in the eye. "When the insanity of your fear consumes you, and the darkness of your imagination floods your ability to see clearly, remember, that which you see emanates from within you, forgive its source, and you are free from it."

Bridges Into the World of Love

Charlie's mind caught on the old man's last words. He thought about the statement of being free from fear, inhaled deeply into his lower lungs, then leaned back into his chair. He looked over at the old man and softly gazed at the tuft of hair protruding from the tip of his nose. "Uhm," Charlie softly spoke, "do you mind if I ask you a question?"

"By all means, please do," the old man replied in a tone as if he felt Charlie's sense of humility.

"When you look to your future, does it end?"

The old man sat for moment staring at Charlie, then said, "Let me ask you a question in answer to that, and see where it leads us," the old man said not as a request, but as a statement.

"Okay," Charlie said.

The old man looked deep into Charlie's eyes, "Have you seen the beginning that you can see the end?"

Charlie sat for moment pondering the old man's question. He shifted in his seat and spoke, "I was born, but I don't really remember it, that's the only beginning that I can believe in. I mean, I know I'm here and that happens through birth, it's what I believe because I can see it."

The old man only sat, staring at Charlie. *Why is he staring at me*, tension began percolating in his groin as he sat waiting for a response from the old man. But the old man only sat quietly, piercing through Charlie with his stare. *Why doesn't he say anything*, he thought. Another thought began to move through his mind, *because he is not here to tell you the answer, he will only point you in the direction*. Charlie was unsure where that thought came from, but chills rippled through his body. He spoke again, "I mean, I believe we are born and we die, and I wanna believe in something more, but I just don't know. I guess I'm not sure what to think. I mean, do we live after we die? Are we eternal or do we only live for a short time?"

"Charlie," the old man said with admonition in his voice. "These questions that you are asking are of no use to you. However, I will fancy your delusions for the time being. But understand, what I am going to say, you may not understand. I will, however, attempt to answer all of your questions, but the result may be that you have even more questions. Questions that you may experience as an even bigger splinter in your mind than the questions you now have. It's not for me to directly answer your questions. Understand that no one can directly answer these questions. Your willingness to face reality is the only direct answer." The old man sat back in his chair, took a sip of tea from the mug and glanced at the pyramids as he placed it back onto the stove.

"Time, right Charlie? It is said by some there was the big bang that brought about life as we know it today. But what framework gave rise to that bang? Whatever it was could be called the Source of the Universe as we know it, for it gave rise to everything that has happened, is currently happening, and will continue to happen. It sourced the thing that banged. It is the cause to an effect.

"Is there something beyond that Source? Beyond that Cause? Who knows, and why does it matter? Coming to know the Source of Life does not happen through conceptualization. These are only doorways out of your self-made prison and into the cavern of the abyss where you stand looking at the bridges out of the World of Fear, then you turn to see the rainbow bridge into eternity.

"Life is happening this instant. Life," the old man paused, "is this instant. This instant, some *thing* is giving you the ability to exist. That something is what You are *existing* within and as, right now. Let's call it Life-Source. Why would we call it that?" The old man paused, then continued, "Because it's what sources your life in this instant, thus, Life-Source.

"Where is your attention point throughout the day, the past or the future? If it's in either it's not in Life-Source which is this instant. If your attention point is not in the only instance of existence, it's focused on a point that does not resonate with life. It's a state of mind that is reactive to the limitation of birth and death, a beginning and an end.

"Yet, that which gives rise to this thing called life is what Life really is. How can there be a beginning and an end to that which gives rise to a beginning and an end as being a possibility?

"That which gives rise to life with a beginning and an end simultaneously contains every possible beginning and every possible end. And the choices made usher the choice-maker down the path walked. And, Charlie, when are those choices made?" The old man paused for a moment giving Charlie time to form a thought.

A look of contemplation washed over Charlie's face, and a moment later his eyes widened as if realizing the immensity of the implications contained in the answer. But before he could speak, the old man said, "Yes Charlie, that is correct, the choices are made right here in this same moment that you and I exist together. And yet, any beginning and any end is only a momentary experience in the transient nature of time. And time delineates the past, and the future; two things that are not experientially now.

"Now is what *is*. It's where Life *breathes* life. And from here, infinite degrees of freedom exist to walk down whichever path you choose. And, if it's the choice to not follow the flow of Life through you, it's a choice destined to know death, an end as you perceive it to be. But is death the end? That is your question correct?"

"Yeah," Charlie quietly murmured.

"So, tell me Charlie, if now is all there is, and you are a stream of life that currently exists now, will you ever be the past? If death of the physical body is the ultimate finality and you no longer exist in a functional capacity, is there no transmutation of energy such that there'll be no part of you existing in the present moment? Will the life that is flowing through you be wiped from existence simply because the body no longer functions? What happens to the energy that is currently permeating the body? What happens to the light of awareness that is currently paying attention to these words? What of the awareness that can come a decision in a situation? Does the body

85

exist as a foundation of this awareness, or is the functional scope of this awareness founded on a framework that is decoupled from the body? Contemplate it Charlie, what happens to the most essential part of you upon death?"

Pausing only momentarily for Charlie to form a thought, "Do you see the implications of what I am saying Charlie?"

Charlie shifted in his seat and softly said, "I think so."

The old man picked up the cup of tea, stared at the image of the pyramids, and then starred into Charlie's eyes with the intensity of a laser. "Charlie, there is no doubt when seeing Truth. If you see the reality of what I am saying you will feel it resonate in your body as love, or as an urge to purify yourself. What are you feeling in your body?"

Charlie shifted in his seat and slowly spoke, "Well, I'm feeling very calm actually."

"What else?"

"My hands are kinda buzzing, and, my uh, my feet are all tingly."

"Okay, describe the sensations in your chest if there are any."

"Well, there's this, this uh, this… well, it's like a, an openness, a space with nothing there but at the same time something powerful is definitely there."

"Take a body picture of this Charlie, let this experience soak into the memory of every cell of your body. Let your DNA breathe in this experience. Let your awareness observe this experience. Sit there for a moment and just continue to breathe deeply, slowly, and notice yourself. Let your inhale open your stomach and let your exhale go. Relax into this feeling."

Charlie's eyes drifted close, his head slowly sank forward, his arms softened and his hands fell into his lap.

"That's it," the old man said. "Just breathe and *feel* the feeling."

For the next several minutes, Charlie drifted deeper and deeper into a conscious relaxation while the old man instructed him into the center of his heart.

"Be in the center of your head and put your attention point in the middle of your chest. Breathe. Feel the feeling."

Charlie's body began pulsing with penetrating warmth. From the center of his chest, a smooth undulating rhythm of purity flowed. He began to taste a sweetness in his mouth, and smelled the aroma of vanilla flowers.

"That's it, feel the feeling," the old man instructed.

Several more minutes passed with supreme silence. The old man sat intensely inside himself holding a vast space of emptiness while Charlie sank deeper into the ocean of crystal purity in his heart.

"Alright now Charlie, begin to move your toes and fingers and bring this depth of being into your body. Slowly now. Breathe. Be in the center of the head and stay focused in the middle of the chest. Let this energy move through you. Deep breath now. Move your arms a little, now your legs."

The old man continued instructing Charlie to integrate the energy into his body. "Take another picture Charlie. Instruct the cells of your body to remember this experience, let your DNA breathe this energy in completely."

Charlie raised his head, his eyes remained closed. "Okay, now Charlie, when you feel ready to open your eyes, do it very slowly. Stay in the middle of your head while continuing to engage focus in the middle of your chest. *Feel* your chest while softly gazing ahead with your eyes and breathe this energy *through* your chest as you exhale."

The old man sat with his eyes closed focusing his attention point on the subtle variations undulating through his energy fields. Charlie began opening his eyes, and as his eyelids cracked a soft smile emerged on his face. "That's it, let your body smile as this energy permeates you thoroughly," the old man said. Charlie tilted his head towards the old man and opened his eyes the rest of the way. The old man opened his eyes and turned toward Charlie. Charlie looked directly into the old man's eyes as they both sat resonating in the deep peace of the moment.

Simultaneously, a deep grin emerged on each of their faces as they took a deep breath in unison. They sat there for a long moment, composed in peace.

The old man gently closed his eyes and turned his head toward the window away from Charlie. Charlie looked down to his hands in his lap, palms up, open and buzzing. As he looked, he saw a soft pale aura around his hands. He took a deep breath.

"Charlie," the old man said still peering out the window through the middle of his forehead.

"Yeah," Charlie replied.

"This is heaven on earth, this is home. Wherever you go, wherever you are, when you are in this space, you are home."

Charlie took a deep breath as he sat in deep stillness, vibrating in vast gratitude. "Thank you old man. Thank you." He smiled, and took a deep breath. "By the way, may I ask you what your name is?"

The old man turned his head toward Charlie, looked him straight in the eye and said, "Charlie, my name is Charlie."

Article 2
Dynamics

Fearlessness, purity of inner psyche, perseverance in the yoga of Self-knowledge, charity, sense restraint, sacrifice, study of the scriptures, austerity, honesty; nonviolence, truthfulness, absence of anger, renunciation, *Happiness*, abstaining from malicious talk, compassion for all creatures, freedom from greed, gentleness, modesty, absence of fickleness, splendor, forgiveness, fortitude, cleanliness, absence of malice, and absence of pride - these are some of the qualities of those endowed with divine virtues...

The marks of those who are born with demonic qualities are: Hypocrisy, arrogance, pride, anger, harshness, and ignorance. There are only two types of human beings in this world: The divine, or the wise; and the demonic, or the ignorant.

The divine has been described at length, now hear from Me about the demonic...Filled with insatiable desires, hypocrisy, pride, and arrogance; holding wrong views due to delusion; they act with impure motives. Obsessed with endless anxiety lasting until death, considering sense gratification their highest aim, convinced that sense pleasure is everything; Bound by hundreds of ties of desire and enslaved by lust and anger; they strive to obtain wealth by unlawful means for the fulfillment of sensual pleasures.

They think: This has been gained by me today, I shall fulfill this desire, I have this much wealth, and will have more wealth in the future; That enemy has been slain by me, and I shall slay others also. I am the Lord. I am the enjoyer. I am successful, powerful, and happy; I am rich and born in a noble family. Who is equal to me? I shall perform sacrifice, I shall give charity, and I shall rejoice. Thus, deluded by ignorance; Bewildered by many fancies; entangled in the net of delusion; addicted to the enjoyment of sensual pleasures; they fall into a foul hell. Self-conceited, stubborn, filled with pride and intoxication of wealth; they perform service only in name, for show, and not according to scriptural injunction. These malicious people cling to egoism, power, arrogance, lust, and anger; and hate Me who dwells in their own bodies and those of others.

Bhagavad-Gita 16.01-18

Chapter 1

Movement: Sloth to Integrity

Sloth

What is the method by which an individual arrives at a morally[6] sound decision? More specifically, in moments of internal conflict, what acts as a function to generate clarity for that individual? In all moments of experience wherein conflict resonates inside an individual, the choice point for a moral decision is at hand. Internal conflict is input to the function of awareness. The function of awareness can only return a value through a decision of willingness. The willingness to be aware is a decision that calls the function of openness. Inside the scope of openness is a functional path to engage honesty, or not. Additionally, the weighting honesty receives is also a function of willingness. The execution of all these functions happens through decision.

Who is the one to make the decision? No one other that the individual who feels the conflict. The responsibility for sane functioning of self must always be found internal to the individual.

Sloth, as defined herein, is necessarily derived from the impasse to nullify conflict by a method known as denial. In other words, when an individual chooses to *not* face the physical, mental, emotional, and spiritual reality of the situation at hand, denial executes, and a thread of sloth is further weaved into the fabric of experiential reality.

The ease with which denial occurs is partly due to the fact that the mind has the ability to see from a uniquely individual perspective,

---

[6] Morality, as defined herein, is the process by which an individual orients to a chosen value system. It is the *process* by which one identifies and implements a value system to guide one's actions.

and subsequently rationalize logical premises based on that perspective. This ability does not necessarily explicate a "universally" valid premise, but it may still be fundamentally logical according to the particular view of reality. To come to a universally valid premise, one must go through an integration process. With sloth, the process of integrity is circumvented by way of denying the contemplative analysis needed to arrive at a more expansive situational context.

To see the situation from a high-level, and abstract the viewpoint requires effort. Tracing that high-level integration through the nuances of the relevant situational details requires the skill of mental abstraction, and a significant degree of effort. The degree of effort requires willingness, as its willingness that initiates the efficacy of the effort. Willingness requires awareness. For some individuals, there is little-to-no awareness of the rationalization process that orients toward an invalid premise of denial. The habituated process of remaining blind to life is just that, a habit.

Yet, if conflict persists in an individual's experiential repository, it is that individual, **and only that individual**, that can re-evaluate the viewpoint with an ever-increasing clarity.

Generally speaking, two basic forms of sloth exist, unconscious and conscious. Of the two, conscious sloth is more insidious in that the individual is aware of the rationalization process; and is not concerned with refactoring the method by which experience is integrated. Unconscious sloth is as a fish in sewer water, and it doesn't know that it's in that type of water.

For the unconscious ones, the input of awareness that initiates the algorithm of freedom generally occurs as severe trauma, although this does not have to be the case. Even still, some choose to remain ignorant for various reasons. Yet, in all situations, internal conflict is the one element that is universal to all human experience that acts as the input for increased awareness. Increased awareness moves toward a willingness to resolve the conflict. Who suffers and actively wants to remain suffering? Moreover, in what ways does individual suffering influence and relate to the suffering of others?

Considering the premise described above, what is a practical example of sloth? Consider a young child, age two, and a father aged 29. The child wakes from a nap one afternoon with a desire to connect with "momma". She soon realizes that her mother is nowhere within the range of her crying. She does soon find her father, but this does not suffice, she continues to cry. What does the father do if frustration arises in him in relation to the given situation?

Three general scenarios exist, 1) He remains frustrated with the child and projects that frustration onto her through various avenues, 2) He becomes present to the fact that he's frustrated and that she doesn't seem to want him or anything he's offering as a solution, and he remains frustrated, which then possibly escalates to anger, or 3) He becomes present to the fact that he's frustrated, and integrates that energy to be more present with his daughter.

The path he takes will be largely determined by the method of rationalization he instantiates. Where he directs his attention-point with what he chooses to focus on will be the input into his mind that either validates the logic of his point of view, or he will see it for what it is, and make another choice; thereby allowing for a different emotional experience for himself and his daughter. Which is the correct solution?

The "correct" solution depends on what his values are and the needs of his child. Is he working on a project that he believes he needs to complete and is of more importance than his child's experience *and* his relationship with his child? Does he believe that his child's current experience is just as important as his? Does he desire to give his child the space she requires to fully process her emotional truth? What are the values he *wants* to uphold, and what are the values he is *actually* upholding?

If he blindly reacts to her experiencing her emotional truth, and quickly replies with, "Quit your whining," in some way, he is not present to the totality of *his* emotional experience. If he was, he would understand the necessity for the space to fully process emotions without suppressing or repressing them. He may want to offer her an alternative mode of expression, but if he in any way is not fully present to his emotional experience in the moment, he cannot offer her the space that he is not giving himself. This is a form sloth.

In this situation, many options exist, and many possible effects could result. One option could be that he does not give his child the space to fully process. He moves to squish her emotions by uncertain means, and in due course, does not resolve his baggage that he probably still carries from his childhood. In this way, he is likely giving his daughter the residual trauma he experienced as a child and is perpetuating the ignorance of emotional dysfunction. The choice is his, and his alone, to resolve the trauma that still resonates in him from his life so that he can offer his child a brighter future. What will be the motivation for him to face the situation more directly without shying away from all that arises in him due to his being uncomfortable with that which arises?

Integrity

If an individual is faced with certain alternate directions that necessarily conflict and may in fact be mutually exclusive of each other, by what method does that individual work out the solution? A solution to conflict of any sort, whether internal or external, lies in the precise identification of a hierarchy of values.

The conscious mind, with its many functional capacities, can generally focus on one thing at a time. It can jump from one thing to another with extreme rapidity; yet there is always at minimum, one context that is currently in the centrality focus. The degree to which an individual is able to mentally abstract is the degree to which that individual is able to hold a higher perspective, and thereby precisely identify a hierarchy of values. A higher perspective always holds all lower order perspectives. This is the innate nature of a hierarchy. This also sheds light on the reasons as to *why* it is imperative to precisely identify a hierarchy of values.

What single value sits at the top? What value is supreme above all other values? These questions are not intended to imply an answer. They are intended to be used as tools for contemplation and introspection toward the identification of a value, any value, which is true, valid, sound, just, and is the pre-eminent value-space of the implementation of all other values.

Integrity cannot arise when an individual holds as equal importance two values that are diametrically opposed to one another. Two values, when one implicitly excludes the other, held inside one's being, is the functional space of conflict. The resolution to which, is, a higher value that rises above and sees both perspectives but does not necessarily apply to them. The value supersedes the conflict.

In the given situation where one value is at conflict with another, the turmoil of the situation may seem to be important. But always with evaluation and identification of a higher more integral value, the importance of lower order peculiarities dissolves. What arises is a clarity that allows for a choice to be made that aligns with all things, while simultaneously allowing for differing perspectives. Integrity does not compromise values, it elevates them.

What is a practical example? Consider again a father with his child, but this time, his son. The given context is such that the father grew up in a context where emotional expression was not necessarily valued and generally shunned. Growing up with and integrating that methodology into his way of being, he saw the flaws in it early on in his journey of becoming a father himself. With his son, he felt it was important to offer him a more integral way of being as a baseline foundation for emotional expression. Yet, in him still lingered the long-repressed anxieties of rage, anger, and various other emotional instabilities. So, what is he to do in a situation where his son is appearing as a threat to the well-being of his other children?

Integrity assumes that he has his, his son's, and his family's best interest in mind. Given his path in life and the current situation, he does not desire to punish his son, yet, he feels strongly justified that punishment is due his son for attempting to hurt his family. One emotion moves in one direction, the other moves in the exact opposite. The logic that rationalizes actions can very easily be concocted to support either case. What are his higher values, and how does he align to them, or not?

Integrity implies integration. An intellectual value system is only effective insofar as an individual is willing to embody the values in that system. An operational value system is the system that is currently operating in the individual as a *way of being*. The father has declared he shall not punish his kids, but rather, positively discipline them when need be.

If he reacts and moves with the anger he feels when he perceives his son as a threat, and promotes logic to justify actions of punishment, he has specified that those actions are in *direct opposition* to what he desires to offer his son as model of interacting with others. Thus, he must come to a value that gives him the internal space to neutralize conflict in himself, so as to move with a more positive approach to discipline. What value does he choose? Said another way, what value does he *move* with?

In this case, he chooses to focus on his breathing. For him, the value of breathing is such that it acts primary to all other worldly values. Without breathing, he cannot offer his son anything. Breathing is both a conscious and unconscious activity, it happens regardless of an individual controlling it, as well as offers an individual a certain degree of control with it. Thus, for him, to focus on the primacy of breathing acts as a higher value in all situations regardless of what the situation may hold. In this way, it gives him the space to neutralize his internal space so as to more proactively move into a way of being that lines up with the value of positive discipline.

The prerequisite in his movement to integrate his way of being is the willingness to act in line with the values that he has identified as moral. In this case, guidance for his son that honors himself, his son, and his family, as well as his son's potential future children, and his children's children. What is the form of discipline the father chooses to enact? To invite his son to go for a bike ride while holding the internal space of gratitude that his son is in his life. What is the result? Without being prompted to do so, his son apologizes for his behavior and seeks reconciliation with his family unit.

Chapter 2

Movement: Greed to Abundance

Greed

> A disciplined person, enjoying sense objects with senses that are under control and free from attachments and aversions, attains tranquility.
> One attains peace, within whose mind all desires dissipate without creating any mental disturbance, as river waters enter the full ocean without creating any disturbance. One who desires material objects is never peaceful.
> Krishna

Isolation is apparent in a realm where a perceived separation between objects exists. By necessity, the function of greed operates from a basis of lack as the predominant paradigm, or point-of-view. As an individual looks outward from the control center of one's own awareness, the movement to focus the attention-point on that which one does not have, or could potentially lose, establishes the framework that allows lack to exist as an experiential reality. This movement of focus, as always, is controlled by the choice of the individual.

The consummate result of a perspective focused on what-is-not tends towards a justification of the apparent isolation of separation. Only from this basis of separation can a consuming fear arise.

It is this primal fear wrought out by the justification of apparent isolation that tends towards the somatic "necessity" to hoard value. When the somatic necessity inspires a movement to hoard values is operating in one's psyche, the tendency toward a disconnected relationship is reinforced. The somatic necessity to hoard feeds the tendency for disconnection. Actions motivated from the basis of disconnection acts as a feedback loop, further intensifying the experience of isolation, and ultimately, fear.

If, by way of the function of sloth, an individual remains unwilling to face the depth of this fear; attempting to cover over the feeling will be the pre-dominant tendency for the individual. It matters not what is sought to cover over the feeling, only that the action is to *not face*. Whereas facing reality is the common denominator of all virtue. The *not* facing of reality is the common denominator of all vice. Greed is no different.

For example, consider the businessman who implements strategies to expand profit at the expense of both the employees used to produce the goods and services, as well as at the expense of the socio-ecological environment.

If the strategy of the individual engaged in business focuses only on reducing the bottom line in order to maximize profit without regard for the integrity of all factors involved in generating revenue; the lack of willingness to see beyond the isolation of greed, then tends toward a destructive impetus in society.

Creating a business system, that, at its base, minimally compensates the individuals who are the ones actually producing the value disregards the value of these individuals in the system. Likewise, to produce a value for society, that in due course, implements an unsustainable process, such as removing forests from the planet to strip out all viable value from the land, does not take into account the need for long-term viability in the overall ecosystem. Short term gain at the expense of long-term sustainability is founded in a view of isolation that is fundamentally guided by the view of disconnection that is separation. The layers in these views recursively perpetuate one another.

In the moment of conflict, when a businessperson is contemplating various strategies, and a decision must be made that has the potential for severe long-term destruction; the responsibility is on both the individual who makes the decision to proceed with the destruction, as well as the individuals who choose to transact with such strategies, by way of purchasing the goods and services in the marketplace.

Only insofar as the goods and services are purchased by individuals is the extent to which revenue is generated in the market. Repudiating the ones who produce value at the expense of the larger socio-ecological environmental sustainability, while simultaneously engaging the market to purchase those same goods and services, is itself, a form of sloth. The value of a free-market un-impeded by the oversight of regulations that serve the elite, is that anyone can enter as a value-creator that obsoletes the old un-sustainable mechanisms.

Forcing the participation of society by means of the threat of violence as the basis for implementing change is by no means a sustainable practice, and is itself founded in greed. The fear of losing the planet's natural capacity to produce abundance, that motivates forced participation in programs is itself founded in the view of separation that sees a disconnection from the integrated whole. Both sides of the business venture, the producer and the acquirer must take stock in the execution of greed in their individual domains. Projecting responsibility onto others when there is individual responsibility not being addressed, is itself a vice, founded in the tendency to *not* face the fullness of the situation. In the situation above, the greed at work is two-fold. One is greed that moves to extract, the other is greed that moves to preserve. Both sides have responsibility.

Abundance

All of that which is extendable, is as such by the nature in which love, or prime energy, operates in the framework of functional existence. Noticing that, in this moment, the current reality exists, it is indicative that a framework underlies the extension of all perceivable forms of existence.

No-thing of form can exist if the fundamental framework is not giving structure to that which exists. Life activity is not possible if the fundamental substance is not moving through the framework. From this base structure and energy, all-that-is arises here in this instantiation of existence.

Insofar as all existence is founded on that which is the primal substance of everything, does everyone who has the conscious ability to become aware of this instant, also have the ability to funnel the primal substance through the personal cosmic construct. Acting as a funnel for the primal substance taps into a source of abundance that is both holomorphic and infinite in nature.

Delusion predisposes an individual towards thinking that a separation exists between this infinite source and the personal point, situated in the space-time matrix as an individual with the ability to choose. By the very fact that an individual has the ability to choose to become more aware of this instant, does the individual also have the opportunity to shatter the delusion that ensnares the mind toward believing separation is real in an absolute sense.

The purpose of the spiritual heart, as a universal function, is to be the gateway of the primal substance. Another word to call this primal substance is love. As the heart opens to the absolute love that underlies and permeates all existence, does the heart also act as a magnifier of that primal substance. As more love becomes available through the magnification by an individual, that love then becomes available to others. In this way, the interior of existence becomes available to the exterior of existence – inner conflict begets world conflict, whereas inner joy begets world joy.

Inasmuch as being a conduit of absolute love is founded on basic universal principles, the experience for an individual is subject to the somatic processes of the individual. The degree to which an individual has developed the skill of tuning into the subtleties vibrating throughout the framework, is the degree to which an individual has the ability to hold the heart in complete invulnerability. Approaching this degree of invulnerability can be, at first approach, a frightening experience. The fear arises by the simple fact that one must be vulnerable with one's heart.

For individuals who have been hurt and have yet to open to the full depth of the pain, being open with the heart is opening it to potential pain. This degree of vulnerability can tend to elicit fear. When an individual is able to be with the depth of pain and soothe it with the source of infinite love that resides as the fundamental nature of one's being, that individual is then able to turn that vulnerability into invulnerability based in absolute love.

The contemplative question that can act as a vehicle towards this invulnerability stems from questioning the core belief that underlie the delusion of separation. The direct experience of the primal substance is the only mechanism to fully eradicate the fog of delusion. Intellectual conceptualization can assist the journey, but the energy and consciousness of absolute love is the only thing bright enough to evaporate the fog.

Herein is realized the value of deep prayer and focused meditation. The intellectual concepts can act as a protection of the internal space necessary to tune into this moment, wherein the love can freely arise into one's experience. Being free of pre-supposition is the power of questioning the core beliefs that form the delusion of separation.

To restate the primary injunction given in the Inroads to this book, "…you will need to let go of all your ideas in order to attain that full communion."

A warning must be given; however, to those individuals who venture down the journey of contemplating the seeming paradox of unity. For individuals who take this journey, any and all notions of control must be eventually abandoned to fully pre-dispose one's heart to being a pure conduit of the highest magnitude.

Operating with the intention to control outcomes and/or individuals, is operating with an isolating intention. This isolation is one of the many appearances of the delusion of separation. Many other traps exist on the journey of fully opening to unity, and the psychological persistence of the individual to be in complete integrity with absolute love is an internal commitment – a decision to be made consistently. This commitment is a sacred contract, and the deeper the commitment, the safer the journey.

To be as freely giving of the primal substance as that which is the source of primal substance, one must come to remove the conditions upon which the heart is opened. Insofar as the individual opens the heart by way of a free choice and opening it for the sole purpose of being in full alignment with one's deepest nature, will the individual know lasting freedom.

To extrapolate this point of "freely choosing love", consider the converse of the example articulated in the above section on Greed. In that, consider the businessperson who is only willing to engage a venture that draws out win-win scenarios for anyone who engages the business strategy. Likewise, consider the consumer of that scenario who is only willing to engage business strategies that have the idea of "win-win or no deal" at the foundation of the strategy.

If this dynamic became the operating paradigm of all individuals engaged in business, in a single moment of time, greed would be eradicated from all business systems, as it would not be operating in the individuals participating in the market. This contextual orientation on the part of the individuals can only be brought about by willingness on the part of the individuals.

If force, in any form, is at work to have individuals engage the strategy, the strategy is itself flawed by the very fact of un-willing participation. Individuals who force participation of others, whether by direct threat, or through by-proxy support of ideas used to persuade others to believe that initiating force is necessary, it is still participating in forcing others.

The responsibility of creating an alternate form of social progress involves stepping into the notion of abundance as a basis of reality. This is an individual pursuit to change the pre-dominant view at work in one's reality. Experiencing the direct result of abundance in one's life requires the integrity to face the situation with full awareness. Sloth perpetuates Greed. Integrity perpetuates Abundance. The choice to re-code one's view of life with integrity of honesty can only be done by a willing participant in life.

Chapter 3

Movement: Wrath to Power

> There is no fear in love. But perfect love drives out fear, because fear has to do with punishment. The one who fears is not made perfect in love.
>
> The Apostle John

Wrath

What can be punished if everything emerges from the same primary root? To punish with motivations of vengeance, or any other motivation, is an intention arising entirely out of the darkness of a self-perpetuated insanity.

Punishment can only appear as necessary if the mind is split in separation. Without that split, punishment is an undeniable non-reality. In oneness there is no punishment, there is nothing to punish. And for the mind writhing in the energy akin to revenge, it is useful to contemplate the distinction between punishment and accountability. One does not equate to the other.

Punishment can only arise from insanity. The insanity is what allows the punishment and vengeance to seem as if the one who is punished *deserves* the punishment. The one who is seen to deserve the punishment is the same cosmic extension of primary substance as the cosmic structure who is lost in the insanity of wrath. Personalities may differ, but the primary root is the same.

As for the contextual premise underlying the nature of punishment; a thought pattern that finds its logical assertions stemming from an idea espousing the inducement of suffering in another, as a means to correct behavior, is at fundamental odds with the nature of that which exists as the source of an object's existence.

Motivations of wrath are a clear indication that the mind is split, and the Light of Truth has been replaced by the darkness of ignorance. The ignorance is dark because the mind chooses to not look at the light. Without light there is darkness. Choosing to not look at the light *in all* is choosing to *be* ignorant, and darkness of mind is reflected.

Wrath can only arise from darkness, and all urges to punish are indicative of the mind being split in the illusion of separation. The interconnected primary structural patterns of the emerging relational matrices of energy cannot be separated. And the Love that gives rise to this "oneness" does not know punishment. Punishment can only appear real to one who chooses the sloth of unwillingness. This sloth begets the confusion and wrath is a resulting consequence. Wrath is an effect to the cause of sloth.

There is no reality to the idea that another *deserves* to be punished. In that idea is the domain of guiltiness. To extend guiltiness to another, rather than grace, is to extend guiltiness to oneself. This extension is the prison of self-made suffering, in which the arrogant choice to support one's self-made insanity locks the doors to that self-made prison.

Releasing personal attachment, by way of grace, to the insane ideology that created the self-made prison of suffering is the only choice available to enter into the domain of Love – the Primary Substance of Existence. A personal attachment to the insane ideology can only exist in one who believes they can subvert Truth and replace it by a false pretense. **The false pretense is the insanity**.

The action to punish, and hold vengeance, arises from false pretenses. If Oneness is seen in all, Truth is extended, and Freedom is blessed. If an individual does not initiate force against another, it is only fair that the same be offered back to that individual. Punishment is not Freedom. Freedom knows not punishment, it is Free. A free society cannot be composed of individuals that punish each other.

Punishment can only arise in a mind that is threatened by the future, or vengeful of the past. In-deed, this devil will surely cause suffering. Yet, this moment stands as the gateway to bliss where suffering is not. Extending the Truth arising from this moment to all that is seen, accepts the Truth arising in all, and wrath has no place there.

For example, imagine a man whose primary focus in life is guided by the motivation to possess power. And the primary vehicle through which he possesses this power is through forcibly penetrating women. Additionally, these women also possess characteristics similar to that of his stepmother. Not necessarily any one characteristic, but they remind him of his stepmother in some way.

An initial question that may arise for one examining the context of this situation might be: what type of woman was his stepmother such that it bred this type of tendency in the stepson? Perhaps that question is not justified, and his stepmother did nothing to breed this tendency, and he picked it up elsewhere. For the sake of this example, however, assume that the way his stepmother was with him did indeed foster the tendency to lust after power, such that taking it from others is, in his view, is a justified means of possessing the value.

From this initial context of possessing power, for the man in the example, it demonstrates as an intense desire to possess power by way of forcing women against their will. To have power *over* women. For years, he has watched himself continually strategize a means to always be in positions of power over women. His mind is completely besought with an implicit sense of lacking power, while simultaneously filling that void with a desire for more power, more control – at the expense of others.

The more he moves in the tendency that degrades, demeans, and weakens the inherent power of women, the more his actions exist in the cycle of disconnection that is brought about by the somatic necessity towards punishment as a form of control, and thereby, having power in a situation.

This cycle holds the perspective of a seeming self-isolation in place, further delineating the logical premise of fear as a justification to perpetuate the tendency he is prone to move with. And if he neither comes to recognize this tendency, nor cultivates a willingness to dissolve it, he will never experience the fullness of personal power that is available in the abundant gift of every living moment.

Inasmuch as his childhood does not bind his future, he need not bind others against their will. But it's all contingent on *his* willingness to face the trauma of his childhood with an open heart, and a commitment to moving in new ways.

The false power he generates by oppressing derives itself from a lack of control. This is where the warning given at the beginning of this book fully illuminates itself. If one is not truly committed to new ways of moving in oneself, and in the world, the result of walking the path of facing the fullness of life will surely result in more suffering for those who have skeletons hidden in closets. The commitment to the inherent integrity of purifying one's consciousness must be the absolute value on this path.

Power

In this moment, arising within, is a force that generates all creation. It is currently resonating. This generative force knows only the generative power inherent to it. The extension of the force is through the extension of will. The will that this force extends, does so, to extend this force to all that is generated. The vector space of the singularity complexifies as the infinitesimal point emerges through the fractalization patterns emerging as the infinite domains of freedom available to the individual by way of choice. It is holomorphic by nature.

The only limitation in the emergence of this force, that is this moment effulging, is the narrated reasoning a mind chooses to believe that supports the motive to *not* give. These narrations arise from the self-made matrix of internal agreements. These narrations are no more Real than the matrix that created them. The only reality to this matrix is the emotional resonance that holds the trauma in one's cosmic energetic structure. Help is available to recover the facets of oneself that remain unhinged due to the emotional disturbance of past experience. One need only be sincere in asking for assistance. It will arrive in due course for a heart truly surrendered to the divine in oneself.

The power of an individual lies in the functioning of the consciousness-to-create. All individuals have the free-will choice to create a false reality of assumptions, in which the narrations regurgitated in the mind arise from that core matrix of assumption.

To know Power, an individual must realize that there is no knowledge anywhere other than in the Truth that generates Life right now. The Truth that generates Life and creates the entirety of all things is the same Truth that composes an individual. Inside, this Power is the power to create accordingly.

Doubt of that power is merely a choice to doubt one's own Truth. This doubt is a perpetuated self-contradiction. It is recursive in nature, and the base case to resolve the infinite loop is the present moment. There is no contradiction to Truth, it is only Truth. If a contradiction appears to be real, a premise in the logic of that assumption is false. That which appears to contradict Truth is only an illusion seen from a lower view of reality. The contradiction that is doubt only serves to further the idea that believes in limitation and fear. Doubt always presents itself as an opportunity for growth – always.

This idea that believes in limitation and fear believes the only power is in the power to control others. Allowing this idea to control the mind is to be out of control of true power. Giving power over to the idea that perpetuates limitation and fear is to be controlled by the idea of separation – Luciferian consciousness.

Power cannot be fully exercised when will-power is not being exercised in the conscious management of one's self. To let the idea that perpetuates separation control the extension of power is to always remain under the control of limitation powered by the choice to be self-contradictory.

Willingness to open into Power must be chosen if an individual desires to know Freedom. This willingness is all that is required by an individual. **This willingness is the extension of personal power**, and when power is extended in true form, it is always in line with Reality, and it increases into infinity.

An unquantifiable degree of power in the universe is exercised by sentient beings when they exercise the consciousness that is choice. An individual must give is the willingness to open into that Power.

The example of the man lost in the lust for power-over women need only turn inwards to integrate the feminine in himself. In doing so, he will undoubtedly arrive at a source of power that is altogether more significant than anything he could extract from others. Touching on the emotional centers of his lower experiential reality will begin to nourish the wounds of his past. In due course, as he cultivates the courage necessary to face the emotional resonances constricting the flow of personal power in his life, he will assist his cultivation of willingness to face that which needs faced.

Persistence and dedication to purity will be his allies in the confrontation of the false premises that await him on his journey. The degree of skill he wields with the Sword of Wisdom depends on his commitment to being a conduit for the higher order of love permeating everything. Holding himself, and his stepmother, in the grace of innocence while forging his path of forgiveness will work to remove those false notions from his path before he arrives to confront them. The invulnerability cultivated in one's heart, by way of surrendering to the absolute of unconditional joy is a power of transformation that is without measure – the magic of true miracles

> I assure you, if you had faith the size of a mustard seed, you would be able to say to this mountain, 'Move from here to there.' And it would move. Nothing would be impossible for you.
> Yeshua

Chapter 4

Movement: Envy to Honor

Envy

The envious one's move in a self-reflection of lack, such that an intention to undermine another takes root in the individual. The seed of lack, if allowed to grow, becomes envy. Experiencing lack, in itself, is not envy. Intending to fill a lack by subjecting another to mal-intent is a movement of envy.

The formation of malicious intent directed at another, no matter how subtle the intent may be, is an indicator that envy may be at work. Merely wishing to possess the same attributes another possesses is not envy, though it can lead there if dwelt therein.

Seeking to obtain a treasure and doing so with a malicious intent based on undermining another, generates a spatial domain of conflict. If the intent one holds for self-experience is to move towards a more joyful state, decisions motivated with malicious intent act counter-productive to the intent of joy.

Neither is it possible to seek Truth, nor find peace, when the allocation of one's mental focus has not moved beyond the density of generating conflict. Logical justifications promoting the validity of conflict can be rationalized when a premise has been established. If, however, the premise is only inclusive of a narrowly defined spatial and/or temporal point, the logical justifications that rationalize conflict are only valid insofar as the premise itself is held as the contextual frame.

The ability to move out of envy must necessarily be accompanied by an awareness that moves beyond the scope of the premise supporting the conflict. In the case of envy, *what* another possesses acts as an opportunity to move to a deeper level than the external gratification of the desire.

Inasmuch as the movement of envy through one's biological construct can produce conflict in the world, so too can the movement to deny oneself the experience of what's underneath the desire. Simply avoiding the feeling of envy out of guilt will not suffice.

The willingness to open to a deeper level of awareness is a decision in being honest with oneself. The effect of such a decision is a realignment of paradigms, thereby altering the bio-cosmic disposition that moves about in reality.

Consider two colleagues who both apply for a position that would result in a promotion for one. Of the two, one is fearful of not getting it because he believes he is competing with someone he perceives as possessing a set of skills more qualified than his own. In spite, he moves to perpetuate rumors that effectually denigrate his colleague's moral character, but rumors that are factually false.

Besought with the compulsion to disparage his colleague's character, he finds himself in a position of moral dis-integrity. As he allocates his focus on the disparaging narrative and continues constructing strategies that have him move in these ways, the projections he perpetuates will only ever see to the limit of the premise that he can only win by tearing another down.

And in as much as he is willing to generate a self-awareness that allows for a dissolution of that false paradigm, is the extent to which he will know freedom. The prison of fear in which he finds himself is a prison entirely of his own making.

Honor

Standing in this moment and seeing the inner essence of oneself, while giving it to all is the blessing of Honor. This is the premise of the "I-in-I". The activity involved in this movement of

Honor is a conscious activity; an individual must awaken to this extension if Honor is to *guide* that Being.

As with all guidance, the movement of honor requires choice. To consciously choose honor is to be present to the value emanating from within. Giving the blessing of honor that arises now, to others, is to free others from their self-made hell.

There is no possibility to *be* free while projecting a prison of suffering onto others. Seeing others in any way other than in the honor of Unconditional Love does not enter into Freedom – it cannot. How can it when freedom exists only in the unconditional domain that is the primary substance of all existence – Love?

What is there to gain in the movements of suffering? What could possibly be the benefit in suffering the chains of hate? Is it retribution? Why is the return of punishment required to know freedom? Punishment can never lead to freedom; relative satisfaction, maybe. Freedom is an existence beyond relative satisfaction. Satisfaction in the punishment of another is a movement of perpetuating insanity.

To perpetuate insanity in any form is to not know joy. To exist in the experience of fear is the attempt to subjugate the essence of True Self beneath the arrogance of a self-made ideology of insanity as the ruler of reality. Such an illusion never knows honor, maybe pride, but never honor.

Releasing the heart into the movement of honor is *freedom*. As this movement of honor flows through the heart, the expansion of the domain of love increases. In the increase of the vector space of love is the anchoring of Heaven to Earth; a change in the basis.

Allowing the insane ideologies of separation to keep this anchoring from occurring allows for anchoring of Hell on Earth. Introspecting upon the circumstances of the Earth, in which war has been waged for countless years all over the globe, it can be seen that many Beings have promoted insanity as the ruler of their reality. If

Honor was *honored*, war would have no place to manifest. The point of this statement is to reflect within, with a greater degree of awareness on that which generates insanity.

When Honor is honored, the opening of Love in the domain of an individual's mind and heart arises. When the vision of Love is seen and embodied, nothing but Love *is*. In that moment when nothing but Love is, all Beings are seen in that Love. Cultivating a willingness for this shift of paradigms to occur must also include a willingness to surrender anything and everything that holds one from this state of joy.

Insanity has no foothold to exist in the one who *embodies* the spiritual love that permeates everything. Validating another's insanity by seeing it for who they are is to *not* see the Truth of who they are, and in that moment, Honor is no longer honored.

Honor can only be given now. Bowing in the presence of the Self in all, is a knowing of the Freedom of Love.

Consider again the two colleagues seeking promotion to a new position. And of the one possessing a set of refined skills that would dispose her to being more qualified for the position, what is her response to knowing that her colleague seeks to disparage her character?

Understanding that her integrity is of her own making, she chooses to see the rumors as they are, without factual merit. And as such rest in the knowing that through transparency, the truth of the situation will be revealed. She neither fears the rumors, nor resents the gossip speaker. She understands that if the position were to be given to the one concocting false pretenses, the organization for which she is employed is not of the moral integrity that deserves her energy. And thereby, she would have no issue moving in the honor of finding employment that aligns to her values.

Chapter 5

Movement: Lust to Sex

> Sexual impurity lies at the root of all individual and societal woes.
> Author Unknown

Lust

An orientation of sexuality that either thrusts or extracts erotic energy with an aggressive posture or duplicitous intent, without considering the full experience of one's partner(s), is a lustful orientation. The movement is itself destructive to the energetic integrity of the cosmic structures of all parties involved.

Operating from lust is a movement lacking consideration for the integrity of self or others. As such, the movement resolves to perpetuate energy signatures that lack an interior alignment of the energy constructs available within oneself. Both the operator and receiver of lust-empowered actions are subject to the influence of these misaligned energy signatures.

Take, for example, the experience of a young boy; whose introduction to his sexuality is losing his virginity through drug induced violent sexual abuse, where he proceeds to immediately repress the trauma out of his conscious memory. Followed by becoming addicted to pornography beginning at age 9. And whose most erotic sexual fantasies are to repeat what was done to him on girls of his peer group and younger, have dominating sex with older women, and to be forcibly penetrated by older men. All while not understanding why he is this way due to repressing the adverse childhood experience; such that his view of himself is that he is inherently depraved.

Now imagine that this sexually oriented context is what he experiences from adolescence, through puberty, and into his early adult life; where pornography is the only safe outlet for his sexuality.

With that premise and contextual example established, the questions that follow can be used to inquire into the premise of this section: *sexual impurity lies at the root of all individual and societal woes*. And from this, extrapolate the practical application to various other sexual orientations.

What is the young man to do with that contextual orientation for his sexuality in the moments when lust courses through his groin? Should he allow himself to make rationalizations justifying the perpetuation of any form of that insanity? Is there any rationalization that would allow for perpetuating the paradigm thrust into his life; such as rationalizing that it's "okay" to view various forms of pornography that perpetuate, to any degree, what he was subject to?

How is he to behave in society, where his erotic sexual desires are to **never** be acted upon? Who is he to turn to for guidance when the moral standards he has been given are standards that specify masturbation as a mortal sin; a sin for which *he will live an eternity in hell for if he dies with that mark on his soul*? How shall he speak about his experience when the criminals who receive society's most vile hatred are the criminals who have acted in the intent of the sexual orientation that was forcibly imposed on his consciousness?

What is he to do when society all around him offers narratives that tell him he is a depraved and worthless being?

Restating these questions as a formal premise; the context an individual uses to *orient* to a particular aspect of life-experience, by necessity, places constraints on the paradigm used by the individual to navigate those life-experiences.

The context of lust limits the scope of the relational-space to a base set of parameters; and as such, the life experience constrained by lust limits the scope of experience for the individual to *that* context.

Inasmuch as lust dominates the paradigm, is the degree to which it is not possible to see beyond the external object of one's own satisfaction and pleasure. Contextualizing objects of pleasure only for one's own satisfaction is entirely self-centered. The contextualization does not allow for the consideration of anyone else involved. Only insofar as another object needs to be present in a given capacity to satisfy the context of lust, does lust traverse a relationship.

The more the idea of enhancing another's experience is taken into consideration, the less lust dominates; and thereby, the various forms of insanity promulgated by lust-filled actions. But this is only if the relational-space is based on the absolute of consensus. The moment consensus is not full, enhancement of the experience begins to diminish.

Lust, as a tool for coercion and manipulation, is the lowest form of power available to humanity. Subjecting others to the influence of these primal energies without consent, or even more insidious, without adequate physical, mental, and emotional maturation that enables proper consent, resolves only to perpetuate suffering in the world.

Likewise, luring others by *false* pretense into being a subject in the storyline of lust, also resolves to perpetuate suffering in the world. Both, the narratives *offered* to the world that perpetuates these forms of insanity, and the active *consumption* of these narratives, are each a mechanism by which the insanity perpetuates. And the rationalizations that allow for such perpetuation are the false notions ("demons") ensnaring one to the lowest forms of personal-power extension.

Increasing awareness of the sexual orientation that predisposes experience to a certain type of interaction is the single most powerful opportunity for a *change of basis*. The moment of orgasm will reveal unconsciousness and thereby tend toward increasing awareness. Trying to stop an orgasm moments before climax, for the sole purpose of being in control of oneself, will reveal the depth to which one is truly *willing* to be in control of oneself.

One moment of honest application of being in control of the cosmic process of orgasm is all that is required to reveal the depth of unconsciousness. The intensity to which rationalizations are construed to justify the continuation of lust, is the degree to which an individual clings to the insanity of lust.

The question is, is there a more enhanced experience beyond the immediate need to reach climax? How is that potential enhancement of experience realized if there is no honest application of being in control of one's cosmic structure, such that the *immediate need* is never transcended?

> Anyone who restrains the sense but mentally
> dwells upon the sense objects, is called a pretender.
> Krishna

Sex

"Sex" – One word to captivate the mind, body, and potentially, soul. An intimate experience of sensual awareness. Driving the human body.

But what does sex really mean. Any person, who has experienced it to any degree, will have an answer. And yet, what sex is conceived to be largely determines whether or not the fullness of sex is embraced.

In the mind, sex may be seen as dirty, demeaning, and disrespectful. A chore needing to be done. An obligation requiring one to duty. An action taken only when necessary.

And yet, sex can also be seen as a deeply intimate experience between two or more consenting individuals, who, by agreement, have entered into a journey in the sacred embrace of sensual exploration.

The question is, is it possible to re-contextualize the deeply physiological paradigm known as sex?

In a formal sense, one possible finality of the sexual intercourse played out by the human species is the generation of life – procreation. Combine one sperm to one egg, a zygote is formed. The continued growth of that zygote is a person with a disposition toward free will – the ability to choose.

Aside from that finality, what else does sex imply? What are the more subtle aspects which are not so easily identified? Think of the emotional vulnerability, and resulting intimacy, that arises between a man and a woman.

What about the intimacy cultivated between two individuals of the same gender? Is their homogenous intimacy as valid as the intimacy of a heterogeneous type? Who can really tell another person that his, her, or their experience of the connection inherent to sensual intimacy is not valid?

The body experiences a felt reality. This is a basic truth. Attempting to invalidate the emotional connection cultivated between individuals, regardless of gender, is an attempt, by the very nature of the premise of the argument, to invalidate the sensate experience of the one making the argument. To deny another's reality is to deny one's own reality. The journey to invalidate emotional truth is left only for those who attempt to claim control over others.

To arrive at a sense of clarity around the questions arising from sexual interactions, a developed ability to sense the depths of the subtleties inherent to the process is necessary. The male dog whose nose runs into the pheromones of a female dog in heat tends to lose all sense of his more "rational" way of being. The same is true for a male deer during the breeding season.

Is the same true for a human male? Does he lose his more "rational" ability to sense and respond to the reality in which he finds himself? And what about a female? Does the "urge" to be connected in mutual desire affect her ability to think clearly and sense the deeper aspects of herself?

If the *urge* to reach climax is such that everything else becomes less relevant, including the experience of the other person involved in the sexual act, how then does one gain the ability to embrace the deeper aspects of the sexual interactions?

That's a potentially heavy question for one who may not be willing to face the deeper aspects of the question. The important thing to note is, that the one who has the ability to ask the question, and remain facing the paradigm shift it implies, is the one who has a seed of the maturity required to make the shift.

And yet, even before fully facing the paradigm shift, one could consider if the question is a fair question to ask? Who says that a more developed maturity is a goal worthy of pursuit in the context of sexual intercourse? Evaluating the worth of developing maturity, as a goal, is part of the reason in asking the questions related to sensing the deeper aspects of sex and remaining to *face the journey* involved in answering it.

Assuming that an individual has arrived at the place where a deeper experience of life is *worthy* of pursuit, then the *opportunity* to re-contextualize sex *becomes available*. And assuming that an individual has made the decision to enter this journey toward greater maturity, the question must be asked; what is sex?

If it has been determined that the main purpose of sex is more than reaching climax and "getting off", then what is the purpose? Maybe that question in itself is not an adequate question to ask if the journey involves arriving at the understanding, only after significant sensual inquiry and practice has occurred.

To replace one concept for another without any direct experience has a tendency toward diminished meaning and understanding. Direct experience has a tendency toward full communication of meaning. If the more important goal is to develop a more significant maturity, it is reflection upon one's experience that tends to facilitate the teaching.

To state it clearly, the purpose of the words in this section are not intended to offer a conceptual understanding of sex. Nor are they intended to articulate an assumption of what an individual will experience on the journey of increasing maturity through sexual re-contextualization.

In reality, these words will be meaningless to the reader who has not, in some way, arrived at this place already. These words are intended to evoke a deeper curiosity about self, sex, life, and relationships.

The presumption of these words is that intimacy and maturity are values the reader holds as valid. If intimacy and growth are not values, the questions composed in this section will probably lead to a dead end. Only if an innate desire to move beyond animal tendencies is cultivated by the individual, will these words have the opportunity to be as water to a seed.

Consider the young man of the last section on lust, in which his contextual frame for sexual interaction was such that he knew his sexual desires were to never be made manifest in reality. What if he was never able to re-contextualize that frame, and thus, grow beyond it? What would the somatic experience of his sexual reality entail?

If, however, he was able to cultivate a *willingness* to grow in the depth of *consensual* enjoyment, such that *it* was more significant than the desire to operate in the orientation of sexuality imposed on him, what would be *possible* for his life?

The result returned from *orienting* to a view of others only as objects of sexual satisfaction, by necessity, shows to the individual the reality that others are there to be used as subjects in fantasies. If, however, the view of objects in space-time is re-coded toward a construction that orients one to the reality of internal *synthesis* in oneself and others, then a new domain of sexual experience can be allowed to *emerge*.

Insofar as an individual has attached the energy of sexuality to the external constructs being the aim, or thing to pursue, for the satisfaction of one's sexual appetite, will be the extent to which the individual is able to elevate in consciousness. Viewing external constructs, as a *goal* of happiness or satisfaction, will always imprison one to *that* domain of activity. Inasmuch as one has begun to construct a view of internal sexual integrity, will be the extent to which the individual is able to rise in the energy of creative potential.

The stated premise herein: internal sexual synergy is the single most important pursuit an individual can endeavor to master.

> If you bring forth what is within you, what you bring forth will save you. If you do not bring forth what is within you, what you do not bring forth will destroy you.
>
> Yeshua

Chapter 6

Movement: The Choice

> At some point you're going to have to make a choice. And that's what life is, life is choices.
>
> Timothy Morris

Choose With Wisdom

Invariably, every moment of suffering or joy distills down to one choice. This choice, as it exists for everyone, is a paramount decision in life, and the necessitation of this decision cannot be underestimated or overlooked if joy and peace is the goal.

Furthermore, the choice is an ever-present algorithm of geometrical expression. In every moment the choice is made, it forever alters the coordinate reality of the time-space continuum, not only for the individual who chose, but for the entire universe that houses the individual as well.

The mathematical nature of this choice is such that, in every instance the choice for joy and peace is chosen, the solution to the equation exponentially increases the infinity of potential allocated as the foundation of reality.

In other words, giving love expands the capacity of love's potential to an infinite degree.

There is never a moment when the choice to love does not exist. As defined herein, a concept of "space" is that it exists as a grid of three axes converging at a center point — three dimensional planes of front-and-back, left-and-right, up-and-down. The fourth dimension is always the moment of choice. In every moment an individual recognizes that a choice is present, that individual is living in the fourth dimension. When no choice is seen that individual is living in the rigidity of the third dimension.

Recognizing choice is recognizing the movement of time's hand. Time, as it exists in clocks, is a measurement of reality's propagation. It takes 10 minutes to hard boil eggs. And yet, the actual boiling of the eggs exists in reality – the present moment.

Coming into the awareness of breathing every breath as a conscious volitional action, aligns one's physical-mental-emotional-spiritual framework up to the fact of Life's present-tense. The choice is always present. *Seeing* the choice is the journey.

What is the choice?

The choice is to perceive life from a self-constructed ideology, or to perceive life from an inherent wholeness of divinity[7]. There is never a moment when the inherent wholeness of divinity does not exist. And there are moments when the self-constructed ideology is obliterated by the inherent wholeness of divinity. Illusion is the self-constructed ideology. Truth is the inherent wholeness of divinity.

The choice is not merely mental, although it involves the mind. The choice involves the entire spectrum of light interpenetrating all the fields of consciousness that exist as an individual. Each individual soul is made in the image and likeness of the primal template – the Creator soul – Christ. Remembering this fully is the end of the journey and the purpose of the choice.

There is never a moment when a soul cannot enter the radiance of the Creator's domain. Believing that it's not possible to enter this domain is the self-constructed ideology of separation that is the "fall" of mankind. The fall and the ascent of mankind exist simultaneously as a choice. Humanity still exists in the Garden of Eden; some simply

---

[7] Divinity refers to the primal aspects of reality that have always existed as the framework for the existence of existence. What those primal aspects are is beyond the scope of this book.

choose to cloud this fact by a self-perpetuated hell of misery and suffering – eating the apple of the knowledge of good and evil.

What is evil in its truest nature? Nothing. What is purely divine in its truest nature? Everything. To see something as good and another thing as evil is to eat of the apple of the knowledge of good and evil. Where is the point at which all things converge into unity?

The original sin that cast humanity out of the Garden first happened many years ago, and it has been continuing to happen up until the present day. Only when every soul on the planet chooses to stop eating the fruit of separation will humanity fully enter into the Garden of Eden.

Hell, and Heaven exist simultaneously.

Hell exists for those who choose to play the game of Victimhood and believe in the powerlessness of sin as the truest nature of their existence.

Heaven exists for those who choose to play the game of Life and embody the power of love as the true nature of their existence.

The choice is now. But be not deluded into thinking the shift will happen overnight. For some, it may. But for others, the journey involves facing every internal construct that perpetuates the hell and deconstructing it.

Eternity is an ever-present, ever-flowing, ever-living quality of life. Life and death do not come and go with the birth and death of a physical body. The energetic essence – Spirit – of an individual does not cease to exist; it merely transitions between states of being. In the physical universe, energy is neither created nor destroyed. How is it possible for energy to exist as a pre-aspect of reality? If it's not created, what/where/who holds it as an inviolate nature of existence?

Eternal damnation is brought about by an individual's choice to perpetuate insanity. Eternal exaltation is brought about by an individual's choice to embody the light of love. The moments of each day that trigger the patterns to perpetuate insanity are the exact moments when an individual has the opportunity to deepen the sacred contract of being a conduit of love. Embrace the challenge as opportunity.

Love is – the extension of the primal nature to hold the existence of all life as inviolate.

The myriad of ways this choice plays itself out in all the nuances of experiential life are plenty. The doorway to the freedom of love in every situation is the breath.

As one origin story puts it, the Creator gave life to Adam Kadmon by breathing life into him. And in many ways, the Creator continues to breathe life into humanity now in the present moment. Access to the creative intelligence of the entire universe is through the breath.

Coming into the awareness of breathing every breath as a conscious volitional action, aligns one's physical-mental-emotional-spiritual framework up to the fact of Life. The choice is always present. *Seeing* the choice, and choosing it, is the journey.

Article 3
Process

THUS, has it been said by the Buddha, the Enlightened One: It is through not understanding, not realizing four things, that I, Disciples, as well as you, had to wander so long through this round of rebirths. And what are these four things? They are the Noble Truth of Suffering, the Noble Truth of the Origin of Suffering, the Noble Truth of the Extinction of Suffering, the Noble Truth of the Path that leads to the Extinction of Suffering. As long as the absolutely true knowledge and insight as regards these Four Noble Truths was not quite clear in me, so long was I not sure, whether I had won that supreme Enlightenment which is unsurpassed in all the world with its heavenly beings, evil spirits and gods, amongst all the hosts of ascetics and priests, heavenly beings and men. But as soon as the absolutely true knowledge and insight as regards these Four Noble Truths had become perfectly clear in me, there arose in me the assurance that I had won that supreme Enlightenment unsurpassed. And I discovered that-profound truth, so difficult to perceive, difficult to understand, tranquilizing and sublime, which is not to be gained by mere reasoning, and is visible only to the wise. The world, however, is given to pleasure, delighted with pleasure, enchanted with pleasure. Verily, such beings will hardly understand the law of conditionality, the Dependent Origination of everything; incomprehensible to them will also be the end of all formations, the forsaking of every substratum of rebirth, the fading away of craving; detachment, extinction, Nirvana. Yet there are beings whose eyes are only a little covered with dust: they will understand the truth...

Hence, the purpose of the Holy Life does not consist in acquiring alms, honor, or fame, nor in gaining morality, concentration, or the eye of knowledge. That unshakable deliverance of the heart: that, verily, is the object of the Holy Life, that is its essence, that is its goal...

Buddha: The Word;
The Noble Eightfold Path

Chapter 1

Method: Concentration

Managing the Attention Point

Much success in shooting a basketball depends on the focal point of the shooter. If the point of focus in the mind of the shooter is the whole backboard, the ball may indeed hit the backboard, but fail in the purpose of the offensive game of basketball – to put the ball through the hoop. The same is true for an archer, if his intention is to mark a bull's eye, his focal point should then be the center point of the target. The idea is that if the aim is small, a miss will be small; therein, increasing the potential of making the mark.

Finely tuning one's ability to maintain *precise* focus is the intention of concentration. The reasoning that supports the importance of concentration on the spiritual journey, or any journey for that matter, can be most illuminated by taking the example of the young man illustrated in Chapter 5 of Article 2 – *Lust to Sex*.

His ability to re-contextualize his contextual paradigm of sex is contingent upon his ability to concentrate and manage his attention point. If he has insufficient ability to maintain his focus, his roving senses will overpower his attempts to shift the underlying pattern of thought from one paradigm to another. This is only one example of the purpose of concentration. In this example, however, the reason to develop the skill of concentration can be ascertained. The *reason* motivating his need to concentrate and manage his attention point is of the upmost importance – innocence is at stake.

To grasp the full efficacy of concentration, contemplate the young man's life from within his shoes. The key to gaining the insight of concentration, is understanding that the more he is able to hold his focus, and shift his paradigm in every situation where *his* particular lust-pattern arises, the more personal-power he generates in himself. Generating that personal-power depends on his ability to intently focus during those moments his specific lust-pattern is at work. Considering that the pattern has been at work for most of his life, and it can arise hundreds of times a day, developing the ability to concentrate is paramount to his peace of mind.

If he fails; however, and misses the mark, the *sin* of lust is functioning in his mind and body, and he is existing in a state of delusion. If the extent of his miss is only in his own mind, and he perpetuates the narrative, he is perpetuating the thought construct that holds him bound to his suffering. If he moves to enact that thought construct *in reality*, he is potentially ensnaring another in the same thought construct.

In all the ways that individuals move with the intention to be more conscious, concentration is at the basis of that movement. Gaining the "eye of concentration" only for the sake of gaining the eye is an irrational motive. Gaining the eye for the sake of freedom is the purpose. Being able to shoot a basketball with supreme skill only for the sake of shooting a basketball will never enter the domain of being able to shoot a basketball with supreme skill during a game-time situation.

The deluded patterns that exist in an individual are specific to that individual. The application of concentration creates a mental space, an awareness, within which a choice can be made. Being able to focus the mind toward enacting values in situations of intense emotion is, in part, the *value* of concentration.

Center Point of the Mind

In any moment, the awareness of the mind can be found in a multitude of places. The *basis* of the attention point of one's mind is always located in the third eye. However, the *point* of focal awareness can be found in a narrative playing out in one's mind, a physical sensation located somewhere in one's body, an emotion flowing through one's being, the outer expanse of the known universe, or any other place where awareness is found.

That which is lighted with awareness is what the third eye sees. The center of the mind is where awareness becomes aware, and neutral observation is the consequence. The point of view from this place is third-person. When the point of awareness is focused on a narrative in one's mind, and the point-of-observation is removed from the *center* of one's mind, the point-of-view is first person. When a narrative in the mind evokes intense emotional response in the body, generally, the observation is from a first-person point of view. When descriptions of the emotion begin with "I feel…" it is a statement of first person, and the awareness is contained to that space-time location. If, however, the descriptions begin with something akin to, "there is a sense of…" it is typically a statement of third-person observation. Neither perspective is the "wrong" perspective from which to be aware. Third person simply allows for a more neutralized space from which to be aware.

Observing the observed moves the locus of control to the center of the mind. Developing the ability to move the locus of control to the center of the mind is a fundamental skill of concentration.

Exercise 1: Centering in the Brain

Step 1: Lightly scratch the forehead between the eyebrows.

Step 2: Stop scratching, breathe gently, and notice the sensations of the scratching. While doing this, be acutely aware of the physical sensations. There is no need to apply a label to the experience. Simply notice the sensations.

Continue breathing with the mind focused on the sensation for 15 to 20 seconds.

Step 3: Draw an imaginary line straight through the back of the head, and feel for the point where that line emerges from the back of the head that is most comfortable.

Scratch this area of the head in the same fashion as the brow. To sense for the point that this line emerges from the back of the head, it may be beneficial to hold a finger to the point on the forehead between the brows.

Step 4: Find the center of the top of the head. Imagine a tube running down through the center of the head, down the spine, out through the perineum and into the center of the earth. Scratch this point on the crown in the same manner as before.

Step 5: Imagine a line running from the top of one ear to the top of the other. Now move that line forward until a sensation of balance is felt in the stomach, just below the belly button. It may help to hold a finger to either side of the head and lightly scratch. The key is to notice the sensations of the body and *feel* for the point at which balance is felt.

To get a sense of balance. Stand on one foot with both arms extended straight out to the side. Put the mental point in the Navel center and lean side to side, front to back, using acute awareness to sense the balance point. It may help to feel the toes and notice the sensations there as well.

With that sense of balance, bring awareness back to the line drawn from one side of the head to the other.

Step 6: Mentally move the three axis lines until the center point of a 3-dimensional grid space is found in the brain. Put all awareness in that center point. Notice the sensations of the body as this happens. Continue to breathe gently.

This is centering the brain. This can be done anywhere, at any time. At first, practicing this centering technique while operating heavy machinery may not be advisable. With continued refinement, however, this particular technique can become a quick way to focus the mind with a greater degree of efficacy in operating heavy machinery.

Exercise 2: Pyramid of Negative Space

Step 1: Bring the arms up fully extended and hold the hands at eye level joining the tips of each index finger together in front, lightly touching.
Step 2: Join the tips of the thumbs together.
Step 3: Look through the space created by the hands and focus the eyesight *not* on the fingers, *not* on the background, but on the space between the fingers. Whatever is in the background will be doubled, as each eye is processing the background individually, and not as an integrated view.
Step 4: Notice sensations of the body as the focus of attention transitions from the negative space created by the hands, to the hands, to the background, and back to the negative space.
Alternate Method: If physical limitations prevent creating a negative space with the hands as described above, create a frame around space by whatever means available to practice focusing on the empty space between objects.

Exercise 3: Octahedron Mind Space

Step 1: Call to mind the three axes created by centering the brain.
Step 2: Terminate each axis with a point about 6 inches from the center point. This will create a basic grid coordinate structure.
Step 3: Cover each face of the grid structure with a layer of white light, in effect creating an octahedron of space around the head.
Step 4: Allow the mind to explore the interior of the octahedron, noticing the distinction of negative space where there is

no thing residing; as well as the positive space taken by mental constructions. If the mind ventures outside the barrier of the octahedron of light that has been constructed, gently bring the focus back to the interior of the structure.

Step 5: With imagination, disintegrate the objects of positive space, and notice any sensations correlated in the body.

NOTE: Disintegrating the mental constructions is neither bad, nor wrong. Notice any resistance to this particular aspect of the exercise as it may be a place to ascertain where attachments and aversions reside. The action of disintegrating the mental construction is simply an action of practicing the power of imagination to clear the mind. Do not move on to contemplation until there is adeptness to dissolving mental constructions in this way. The emotional aspect of contemplation requires an ability to clear the mind to more fully *sense* and be aware of the root of the emotions. Practicing clearing the mind, and working through any resistance that may arise is a preparation for more intense work ahead. The turtle's pace is recommended in this practice.

Chapter 2

Method: Contemplation

Clear Thinking

Bias, in the formation of mental constructions, is the root of all delusion. Attachment to mental constructions founded on bias is the surest path to insanity. Perpetuating insanity is a process by which an individual imprisons oneself in a self-made cage.

Transcending the confines of limitation ensnaring an individual to a space-time construct requires moving beyond personal bias and into universal principle. Only insofar as a cultivation of willingness to see perspectives other than a personal context will transcendence of pre-defined limitations be possible. An awareness primarily framed by the positional space-time awareness of birth and death of the body will return results accordingly.

Skepticism, at its root, does not allow for transcendence of personal limitation. Skepticism works towards knowledge based on what is knowable only from a personally defined frame. Scientific skepticism is a movement of "seeing so as to believe", and does not allow for the spontaneous creativity of "believing so as to see". Following an internal movement to ridicule things such as "believing so as to see" is indicative of harboring a fear of the unknown. Conversely, only operating out of "believing so as to see", is also a delusion. Proper testing of theories is required to refine the thought process.

One does not have to believe in something necessarily, but suspending disbelief can act as a bridge to a greater degree of awareness. Likewise, if there is no functional merit in an idea, immediately disbelieving may not be the most fruitful movement.

Suspending belief; however, may act as a way to open to new ways of thinking about the given idea at hand without rejecting the entirety of the notion.

Vacillating between belief and disbelief about a particular idea is not clear thinking. Refinement of the conceptual model to align to the universal principles at work in the given situation is a movement of clear thinking.

As an example, many who entertain this book with sincerity will undoubtedly face delusions around what is held as the idea of "God". Some may experience this word with aversion, others may experience it with great fondness. And yet, for others, the word may be of no emotive consequence. Irrespective of the current emotional resonance induced by the word, the importance of clear thinking regarding the concept of "God" ventures into the primal cause of one's present existence. Coming to an unbiased conception of the root of universal personality-extension within an individual frame requires a distinct capacity to transcend the bias of the personal space-time context. When it is experientially realized that the human mind alone cannot fully form the conception of "God", real progress on the path of unbiased thinking has occurred.

Clear Feeling

The progression toward refining awareness of the various emotive resonances fluctuating through the human body must start at the level of skill currently possessed by an individual. And even before that progression can truly begin, a decision to value *clarity in feeling* must be made. To make this decision requires placing importance in the principle of honesty. Without honesty, clear feeling is not possible. The clarification of emotions happens through increasing the degree of self-honesty implemented by the individual.

In the movement to be more honest with oneself, the discipline required to enact a full scope integration of honesty must, by necessity, be both ruthless and gentle. Synthesizing ruthless honesty with gentle honesty will bring forth an inner disposition that establishes a basis of balance. Self-degradation is not honesty. Self-aggrandizement is not honesty.

The journey of integrating honesty at the fullest scope possible does not happen in a day, and it may very well involve seeking professional help to adequately re-narrate one's contextual frame of the self to be inclusive of radical honesty. Once the importance of honesty has been firmly established in one's dispositional outlook, the journey of refining awareness of the various emotive resonances can begin.

In this progression, the more an individual is able to generate the space of interior openness to the emotions, the more the arising and passing of emotions can occur with a reflective mental frame. This reflective mental frame is necessary for contemplation. Becoming consumed by an emotion, such that the emotional experience is predominantly viewed from a 1st person perspective, does not allow for the function of contemplation. Giving space to emotions without the basis of action being motivated by the emotion is necessary for contemplation.

If it is found that there is difficulty generating an interior openness to a certain set of emotions, it may be that this aspect in oneself holds a significant degree of emotional disturbance. **Caution is warranted**. In these scenarios, it may be that these are the spaces where professional help is most beneficial. Unfolding repressed emotions will undoubtedly bring challenge to one's experience. In this process, it is important that an adequate psychological frame is established to be able to fully face the challenge. Framing that psyche without proper guidance can lead to unforeseen roadblocks if not taken with great care. In this care, it is advisable to begin a journey of self-trust, such that trust can be established with a qualified individual in the psychoanalytic process needed to re-contextualize these difficult spaces in self.

Acknowledging a need for help is not a sign of weakness. Rather, acknowledging the need for help is a sign of the resilience inherent to the courage necessary to face these aspects. The repression and suppression of emotions is the more legitimate sign of weakness. Not allowing oneself to feel the depth of an emotional resonance is an action of disallowing full experience. What is it about a certain emotion that a movement toward disallowing the experience a full-cycle process, needs to be the movement. The actions taken from the emotion are not a pre-defined set of actions. The behavior demonstrated with the emotion(s) can be established to be healthy for all in the situation. Consciously suppressing the experience is a statement of the lack of the emotional maturity necessary to be in a situation and allow oneself the full-cycle process. Why set it aside for a later time? It may be clarifying to closely examine the rationalizations that speak to setting it aside. Whom do those rationalization truly serve?

Clear Sensing

Once the zygote is formed in the womb, the physical body is constantly in a perceptive process. There is never a moment when the body is not in a sensate function.

As with clear feeling, clear sensing also requires an interior space of openness to reach a fullness of sensation. Aversions and attachment to certain sensations creates an imbalance in one's view of self. Understanding preference is a more balanced view of self. Always seeking pleasure, and avoiding pain at all costs does not allow for life to arise as it is. Conversely, holding the view that experiencing pleasure is the basis of guilt, and that pain is the basis of nobility acts as a restriction to life arising as it is.

A preliminary movement of clarifying sensation involves the release of tension stored in the body. Storing tension in the body over the long term is a source of pain. For example, clinching the teeth when feeling anger, over the course of a life, can lead to a misaligned jaw structure, and thereby the sensation of pain, particularly headaches. Similarly, if clinching the teeth is an unconscious movement, the residual tension stored as muscle memory after the anger has subsided, can also lead to a sense of numbness.

Numbness, as a function in the body, does not allow for the processing of the human experience. It is necessary to address all areas in the body where numbness resonates to arrive at the function of clear sensing.

Likewise, all areas of the body where there is a lack of functional awareness, it is necessary to address those areas as well. A gauge of functional awareness of the body can be ascertained by integrating a proprioceptive view of one's body. Being able to flex a single muscle, rather than a muscle group, is indicative of having a functional awareness of that area of the body. Working towards the ability to flex singular muscles within a muscle group is a process.

After these preliminary movements are established by an individual, the process of clarifying sensation can occur with more proficiency. At this stage, removing attachment and aversions to certain sensations can be more effective. Without the removal of attachments and aversions, the inner disposition will not allow for the integration of equanimity. Arriving at equanimity is the goal of the journey of clarifying sensation. In the space of equanimity, wholeness can then be brought to experiential recognition.

The infinitesimality intrinsic to the holomorphic fields pervading the manifold of physical space allows for the universal whole in the singular unit. Clarifying sensation arrives at the functional capacity to sense the infinitesimal as the whole. Generating an interior space that allows for experience to arise as it is occurs through equanimity. The release of tension stored in the body is the beginning of a journey toward equanimity.

Synergizing the Functions

Connecting the trinity of *clear thinking* and *clear feeling* and *clear sensing* allows for an operating symmetry in motion. This operative symmetry is known as contemplation.

Cultivating the skill of contemplation is a process. And the more an individual refines this skill, the more the capacity to process experience into functional units of knowledge, integrates itself as basis for an individual's dispositional outlook on life. Wisdom becomes operational.

Being able to frame a proper psychological context around the *sensate* experience of one's *emotive* processes is the synthesis of this trinity. Likewise, being able to frame one's psyche around the *emotive* experience of one's *sensate* processes is a further progression of the synthesis. Being able to experience distinction between the sensate and emotive experiences, in a situation where *both* experiential domains are resonating to significant intensity, is indicative of a refined capacity to contemplate. For example, experiencing explosive anger when hitting the head hard on a low door-jam is a situation where both the sensate and emotive domains are with great intensity. Holding internal space for both experiences while simultaneously moving with proper attention to both requires a *stability* of awareness.

The focal point of each domain of contemplation resides at specific locations in the body. Clear thinking – the center of the brain. Clear feeling – the center of the chest. Clear sensing – the center of the abdomen. Gaining facility in awareness of these three locations is necessary for contemplation to reach maximum efficacy.

Exercise 1: Centering Self

Step 1: Center the brain (see Exercise 1 of the chapter on Concentration for detailed instructions).

Step 2: Center the heart. Similar to centering the brain, the three-dimensional grid structure created around the head will also be created around the heart. Touch the center of the chest, and with imagination, draw a line parallel to the ground and straight through the center of the back between the shoulder blades. This is forward to back. The up and down axis is already established by centering the brain, simply extend the line downward through the perineum. Now visualize a line running from one armpit to another, a few inches below the apex of the armpit. It may help to touch these points with a finger to establish a sensation as a focal point. Similar to centering the brain, terminate the axes and cover the faces with white light.

Step 3: Center the navel. Touch a finger just below the belly button, and visualize a line parallel to the ground running through the lumbar section of the spine. Recall the vertical axis established when running the line through the perineum. Now visualize a line running from the top of one hip to the other. Again, terminate the axes and cover the faces with white light.

Step 4: Sit in awareness of these three spaces for 10 minutes, allowing whatever arises in each to arise as it is. If attention drifts, simply bring it back to the focus of these three spaces. Once an internal space of openness has been established, exercises 2 and 3 can take on a greater degree of functional efficacy.

Exercise 2: Refactoring Questions

Step 1: Visualize the google homepage 2 feet in front of you. Focus on the text box to input the words to search.

Step 2: Visualize 3 lines of energy extending from you to the search box. One from the center of your brain, another from the center of your chest, and the third from the center of your abdomen.

Step 3: With your imagination, input a question, words, or a word into the search box, and press enter

Step 4: Notice yourself return the results. Notice what sensations arise. Notice what feelings arise. Notice what thoughts arise.

Step 5: Experiment with changing the structure of the question and notice what arises as you think through refinement of the question to be a more succinct expression.

Alternate Version: Hold the question, the words, the word, the image, etc. in your mind's eye as you notice what arises within as you continue to hold your attention on the mental object.

Exercise 3: Daily Permutations

Step 1: Focus into the center of the chest, and ask, "What is the most significant block to peace in my life?"

Step 2: Wait till a thought arises with a significant emotional resonance related to your question.

Step 3: Throughout the day, bring presence of awareness to the thought, and notice yourself.

Step 4: In every permutation of this function of awareness throughout the day, take special note of any variances of the emotions or thoughts, while intending for yourself to generate a greater sense of openness. There is what is the block, and there is what is the vehicle to greater peace. Take note of both.

NOTE: This exercise requires having tuned into the emotional and sensate processes that are unique to you. If you find this particular exercise difficult, spend more time practicing the first exercise of **Centering Yourself.** Only after you have developed sufficient skill with adequately centering yourself will the daily permutation of facing your inner blocks to peace bear fruit.

Chapter 3

Method: Meditation

Observation

In a most basic understanding of meditation, it can be defined as a process of observation. This description may seem like an oversimplification of a highly complex process; however, meditation in its *functional* scope is an activity of *allowing* for the input of awareness. Remember the sequence of the algorithm of freedom. Go back and remind yourself of the sequence if you are in question.

What arises inside of meditation, how the meditation is guided, and who engages the process is always different. The functional scope; however, never changes.

Awareness *is*. This axiomatic fact can be resisted. Or, opening to the process of "knowing thyself" can be chosen. It is a matter of one's willingness. The ability to increase awareness of self **depends entirely** on the willingness to move beyond the mental frame that establishes the human body as the *basis* of identity. Reread this paragraph. Allow it space to exist. Contemplate it.

Active Observation

Directing the mental constructs while noticing the resonances in the experiential domain is active observation. In other words, guiding the observation with visualizations can induce certain experiences. Visualizing a pillar of light running through the core of the body can induce a specific experience. Imagination is not only for a child's playtime dream-scape. The ability to generate metaphorical space in the mind is the defining ability of a **creator**.

Generating metaphorical space is the precursor to every idea ever made manifest as a physical construct. Additionally, the metaphorical space given to oneself for the sole purpose of evolving one's consciousness is the primary decision every seeker of knowledge must make.

Until such a decision is made, the evolution of consciousness cannot begin in earnest. Before then, *being conscious* is only a hobby; a part-time pursuit to be tinkered with on the weekends. **Do not expect meaningful results with such a decision.** You are only setting yourself up for failure if you hold the expectation of meaningful results while actually sitting on the fence of equivocation. It bears repeating, DO NOT DELUDE YOURSELF in such ways. This would equate to a form of deceiving yourself. Stop it! Guilt and Shame is not necessary; a **decision** is.

Passive Observation

Neutrally examining that which happens to flow through the construct that is {this} moment is the skill of passive observation. Emptying the mind of the regurgitated content of the day is a process of honing the mental functions towards the sharpness of a razor. Irrespective of possessing any skill in passive observation, the process of aligning to a still mental space requires only persistent intention. A flame of integrity is required to forge the sharpness of this skill. A sword of the sharpest edge is not forged with only one swing of a hammer, it requires intense heat, much compression, and at minimum, an intention to see the process through.

Succumbing to the excuse of being unable to still the mind may be an adequate excuse for the hobbyist on the journey for greater self-knowledge. But for one who desires to *know thyself* like a drowning man desires air, the intention of stilling the mind even in the depths of a consuming rage will be ever present. Nothing will be as important as one's own volitional ability to still the mind in any situation. For until such skill has been acquired, the seeker can rest assured that more inner skeletons have yet to be unearthed.

> There is neither Self-knowledge, nor Self-perception to those who are not united with the Supreme. Without Self-perception there is no peace, and without peace there can be no happiness. Because the mind, when controlled by the roving senses, steals away the intellect as a storm takes away a boat on the sea from its destination – the spiritual shore of peace and happiness.
>
> Krishna

Exercise 1: The Flame of Integrity (Active)

Prerequisite: Proficiency with the *Centering the Brain* exercise for Concentration.

Step 1: Internally locate the center of the brow.

Step 2: Extend a filament of light from the center of the brain, through the center of the brow, to a point 18 inches in front of the head.

Step 3: Visualize the flame of a small fire at that point at 18 inches.

Step 4: Notice the sensations of the body as the flame is visualized. Notice for any changes in sensation, i.e., hot, cold, warm, soft, hard, rough, expansion, contraction, etc. DO NOT put a simile on the sensation, as in, "it feels like…". **Be concise** in noticing any changes in the somatic experience of visualizing the flame.

Step 5: As thoughts begin to arise, visualize the thought as a twig being thrown into the fire. Notice for any changes in sensation.

Step 6: Continue for at least 10 minutes.

Exercise 2a: The Flower (Active & Passive)

Step 1: Choose a flower that has both a fragrance that is pleasing to the body, and is readily available to the moment at hand.

Step 2: Breathe in slowly through the nose with the locus of control centered in throat or trachea. DO NOT suck in through the nose.

Step 3: Allow the fragrance to stimulate the olfactory receptors at the top of the nasal cavity.

Step 4: Breathe out, **slowly,** with the locus of control centered in the trachea.

Step 5: While breathing out, allow the body to inform the somatic experience of interacting with the flower; and notice the sensations of the body. Marinate in this somatic experience induced by the floral essence.

Exercise 2b: The Christ Flower (Active & Passive)

Step 1: Close your eyes and visualize Christ in front of you, looking into your eyes with a gentle smile on his face.

Step 2: Breathe in slowly through the nose with the locus of control centered in throat or trachea. DO NOT suck in through the nose.

Step 3: Allow the presence of Christ's energy to stimulate the nerve endings in the fascia surrounding the muscles. Let the energy pervade the entirety of the body.

Step 4: Breathe out, **slowly,** with the locus of control centered in the trachea.

Step 5: While breathing out, allow the body to inform the somatic experience of interacting with Christ's energy, and notice the sensations of the body.

Exercise 3: Trinity Expression (Passive)

Step 1: Internally locate the center of the **Navel** region. Sense for an area behind the belly button, and a few inches down. Develop an acuity of sensation for this area in your body.

Step 2: Breathe in slowly through the nose with the locus of control centered in throat or trachea. Filling all chambers of your lungs completely. DO NOT suck air in through the nose.

Step 3: Breathe out, **slowly**, with the locus of control centered in the trachea. Emptying the majority of your lungs, to an ease of comfort.

Step 4: While breathing out, allow the body to inform the somatic experience of interacting with this *body* energy center, and notice the sensations of the body.

Step 5: Internally locate the center of the **Heart** region. Sense for an area behind the sternum, a few inches above the center of the chest. Develop an acuity of sensation for this area in your body.

Step 6: Breathe in slowly through the nose with the locus of control centered in throat or trachea. Filling all chambers of your lungs completely. DO NOT suck air in through the nose.

Step 7: Breathe out, **slowly**, with the locus of control centered in the trachea. Emptying the majority of your lungs, to an ease of comfort.

Step 8: While breathing out, allow the body to inform the somatic experience of interacting with this *heart* energy center, and notice the sensations of the body.

Step 9: Internally locate the center of the **Brain** region. Sense for an area behind brow, just above and forward of the ears. Develop an acuity of sensation for this area in your body.

Step 10: Breathe in slowly through the nose with the locus of control centered in the throat or trachea. Filling all chambers of your lungs completely. DO NOT suck in through the nose.

Step 11: Breathe out, **slowly**, with the locus of control centered in the trachea. Emptying the majority of your lungs, to an ease of comfort.

Step 12: While breathing out, allow the body to inform the somatic experience of interacting with this *brain* energy center, and notice the sensations of the body.

Step 13: Remain breathing through the nose, with an awareness of these energy centers in your body, observing and noticing sensation. Do this for a minimum of 10 minutes. If your mind wanders, gently bring it back to an awareness of these three energy centers, noticing sensation. It may be helpful to continue rotating through the energy centers with each breath until a deep sense of each is fully cognized. Play with this movement toward bringing awareness of all three centers to a simultaneous sense of integration in with each breath.

NOTE: This is only a basic meditation that acts a foundation to an ascending multi-dimensional array of energy movements. Without this foundation, the rest of the structures cannot be built, for there is no foundation. As such, **this is the single most important practice to achieve mastery with first**. Go slow, and give yourself the opportunity of being acute in your sense-ability of these aspects of yourself. Repeat this practice as many times as a professional basketball player would repeat practicing of a free-throw (thousands of shots [breaths] a day if needed to acquire adeptness). Do not try to jump ahead if you cannot sit for at least 10 minutes with a simultaneous sense of all three centers in your body's somatic experience. Thinking you "get it" is **not** the same as an acute sense of all three center in simultaneous awareness. This skill is a key that unlocks many other things in your soul.

Chapter 4

Method: Introspection

Orienting the Internal Map

Introspection functions by directing contemplation toward an interior examination of self. Cultivating the intention to *reveal* the primary root intrinsic to personality extension is an optional parameter to the function of introspection, but not required. Holding this intention, however, bestows many benefits for an individual possessing a willingness to face everything and avoid nothing.

As part of experimenting with the Theory of Body Integration, a hypothesis to test is in regard to numbness in the body. The theory states that numbness in areas of the body arises by way of the pain threshold being overwhelmed to the extent that numbness is the result of the sensory overload mechanism. As such, areas of numbness in the body are areas where the function of introspection can bring an increased awareness toward *knowing thyself*.

An avoidance of pain that results in a lack of awareness in oneself neither increases quality of life, nor resolves the root of the issue. If pain is avoided, it becomes a multi-layer composition of disease. Physical pain, emotional turmoil, and mental anguish are the layers.

All the rationalizations that have been established by the individual to justify the avoidance is the core of the mental anguish. This mental construction acts as a formidable blockade to resolving the root of the pain. In some cases, the block may be so formidable that the pain was repressed as a child, and no memory of specific situations are available to examine. Such can be the case with the trauma of childhood sexual abuse.

Repression in such ways makes it exceptionally difficult to isolate the root of the trauma such that it can be resolved. In such cases, a trusted professional with the integrity necessary to assist is often required to uncover the repression, and uproot the core of the trauma.

Orienting the internal map of self-discovery requires *intention*. The orientation happens *by way of* the intention. Introspecting for the sake of introspecting is as an artist mixing paint for the sake of mixing paint. The more an artist holds an intention to discover colors by guiding the mixing with hypotheses, the more color *theory* becomes color *wisdom*. In like manner, the more an individual guides introspection with the intention of self-discovery, the more likely the individual will discover ever greater aspects of self.

Acknowledging that those greater aspects are only discoverable by also having the willingness to face everything and avoid nothing is a prerequisite to the process. One must be *willing* to journey through perdition in order to enter into grace. The journey through perdition does not *have* to occur, but the *willingness* to face it must still be there. In such way, one can be assured of facing everything there is to face to fully embrace a state of grace.

The notion of "I am not worthy" must be eradicated from one's mind. This notion is a delusion – a mental disease. Forgiveness and grace establish the predicates necessary to recognize one's inherent worth. To believe otherwise is both a statement of not having self-forgiveness, and not having a willingness to embrace reconciliation of one's paradigm. Acting in harmony with the unceasing light of unconditional love is a choice. Acknowledging one's inherent value, and by consequence the value of all others, is a choice to remove the idol of death from God's altar in the heart.

Loving God and others cannot reach maximum efficacy with the idol of death, the idol of "I'm not worthy", sitting on the altar of one's heart. Introspection is a vehicle that brings an individual to this choice of accepting inherent worth, or continuing to worship the idol of death. Cognizance of the choice is paramount to living free. Without this cognizance of the choice, an individual is a slave to a master, and knows it not.

With a lack of cognizance regarding the choice to worship death or life, an insidious state of being a slave, while thinking one is free, can result. This insidious internal orientation of self happens to be the state of many individuals on this planet. Out of ignorance, sloth, and pride, these individuals choose to serve the Masters of Death while believing they are serving freedom. Rationalizing the killing of other humans to secure the freedom of a nation-state is symptomatic of this state of ignorance. Rationalizing the death of innocent children as "collateral damage" is another symptom of an individual worshiping the idol of death, and being servants the Gods of Death.

Exercise 1: Whom Do I Truly Serve?

Step 1: Stand or sit in front of a mirror, lights out, with a small candle between you and the mirror.

Step 2: Look into your eyes and ask the question, "Whom do I truly serve?"

Step 3: Remain looking in your eyes for at least one minute.

Step 4: Go to sleep

Step 5: Upon waking up, write down all details of your dreams, paying attention for any name that stands out in your heart as who you serve.

Step 6: Continue this every night for as many nights as needed to get a recognition in your heart related to a Name.

Step 7: Research that name. Investigate who you serve and decide about your continued subservience to that Master, or choosing an alternate Master.

NOTE: Be warned about serving the Master of Ego. Being self-interested is vastly different that serving the Master of Ego. One is oriented toward looking out for your well-being, the other is serving a force of imprisonment. The subtlety in the decision is highly nuanced. Both your True Self, and the Master of Ego are with you every moment of every day. They both look back at you when you are standing in front of the mirror. Choose clearly.

Exercise 2: Who Am I?

Step 1: Stand or sit in front of a mirror, lights out, with a small candle between you and the mirror.

Step 2: Look into your eyes and ask yourself the question, "Who am I?"

Step 3: Remain looking in your eyes for at least one minute.

Step 4: Go to sleep

Step 5: Upon waking up, write down all details of your dreams, paying attention to any particular characteristic of your dream that holds emotional resonance.

Step 6: Continue this every night for as many nights as needed to gain a vision of who you are beyond the physical form.

NOTE: Allow the recognition to be based in your heart, not as an intellectual interpretation. Understanding the difference between a recognition in your heart, and your intellectual interpretation will be facilitated by being diligent about refining your ability to contemplate. Revisit the method of contemplation if you are in question regarding this.

Chapter 5

Method: Integration

> The single most important skill to develop as an artist is the ability to create dimensional space, i.e., depth, width, height, length, etc.; not just literal space with matter, but **especially** metaphorical space, the living creation of the soul.

Integrating Breath

Premise: Mastering breath is mastering life!

Becoming a master of inhaling, exhaling, and holding breath integrates a degree of functional awareness that supersedes all other functional priorities. Allowing the breathing patterns to fall to chance, or unconscious habit, is an action of mapping the decision matrix onto a priority structure with a higher probability of aligning to insignificant valuations of life's priorities.

The more the skill of guiding breath is cultivated by focused intention, the more one's *functional* priorities will shift. They are functional in that these practices alter the way an individual operates "self" in life. They are distinct from *intellectual* priorities that an individual may *think* are important. Functional priorities are *actually* important – the key word here is *act*.

The unique breath pattern intrinsic to an individual's cosmic effulgence arrives at conscious integration through a multifunctional process. The common breath pattern of breathing in, then breathing out, arrives at functional operation through an unconscious orientation to breath. The emergence out of that unconsciousness occurs most noticeably through body integration; specifically, orienting awareness to the somatic release of tension. As tension releases from the body, facilitated by the function of breath awareness, a specific breathing pattern is required by the body for this release of tension. It is a pattern only knowable to each individual through the various functions involved in engaging the process.

Integrating Body

Premise: The body's intelligence receives instruction through intention.

Refactoring the programmatic instructions, the body receives from your belief matrices is an ever-progressive refinement process. Stagnant tension in the body's somatic experience results from a codebase that allows for a buildup of blockages. The primary gauge to begin an attunement towards your body's ability to re-program itself is the breath. Your unique breathing pattern is an alternate code base to operate from.

Use your breath as a vehicle to sense the energy fields that exist as the framework, the foundation, the basis of your ability to exist as a physical construct in space and time. Move the body in micro-movements towards the proprioceptive neuromuscular release of stagnant tension. Balance the structure of the bones in the innate symmetry of the human form.

The spontaneous flow of movement that emerges from an integration of all functional capacities is not an intellectual activity. The intellect can begin to understand this process only after the body has begun to experience the process. It is you focusing the totality of your consciousness on your selected intention that will initiate the process.

Integrating Mind

Premise: Where the attention goes, actions follow.

Conscious action in life is only possible through choice. As you continue to enlighten these words with your awareness, you are using choice as a method to *continue*. The *intention* you hold as you place your *attention* on these words informs both your intellectual and somatic experience. Reading to refute what is presented will produce insight along those lines. Reading to engage what is presented will produce a different type of insight. What you receive from this book is based on two intentions, 1) My intention in writing it, and 2) Your intention in reading it.

As stated several times throughout, the purpose of this book is to point you toward freedom. As such, my intention is to be a guide on that journey. What you bring to the process of engaging this book will largely determine the experiential insight you generate for yourself along the way.

Your ability to concentrate is paramount towards integrating your mind. Allowing your mind to rove without an awareness that it is roving indicates that this is the first integration point to establish. If you find that your mind wanders from thought to thought, or idea to idea, and it keeps you from engaging a more focused breathing practice; you then have an initial goal to work toward. That is, reprioritizing your breath-work by concentrating on it as a primary intention in your operational context.

Your choice to practice is your pathway to achieving your goal. You can do this while you continue to read, or while you engage in any activity – as I have done while writing. Guide your mind's attention. If you're not guiding it, you are leaving it to be guided by the random influences you allow into your life.

Integrating Emotion

Premise: Feeling the full depth of emotions is real freedom.

In simple terms, if you are not able to feel the fullness of the emotion(s) that exists in you, you are a prisoner to that emotion. If it is fear, then you are a prisoner to fear. If it is anger, then you are a prisoner to anger.

Repression, suppression, or avoiding emotions to any degree is a dysfunctional process that will always have *unintended* consequences you are *unaware* of. Being unable to feel anger in its fullness, may look like clenching the teeth in the moment. This may be done in order to arrive at the other side of the situation where the intensity of anger diminishes. The repetition of clinching the teeth, over the long term, may result in a misaligned jaw structure, factures in the teeth, and chronically tense jaw muscles. This state of the jaw may be a root-cause of the skull not resting on the atlas of the spine correctly, resulting in a misaligned posture. The misaligned posture may be the root of chronic pain in the upper back. All this may be a cause of recurring headaches, to the point of migraines. All this tension and pain around the lungs may lead to a significantly diminished breathing capacity.

Though the above example may sound hypothetical in its presentation, the psychosomatic implications of such a scenario did not arrive out of hypothesis. Rather, they arrived out of the direct experience of a certain individual. Understanding the psychosomatic implications of *not* feeling the fullness your emotions reveal correlations to the roots of many processes that may be at dysfunction in your body, as well as your life in general. The relationship of the mental paradigm you use to allow or disallow yourself the opportunity to feel, in fullness, is the psychosomatic connection to your current state of function or dysfunction.

The surest path to an integrated state of health is through alignment in yourself to a paradigm that allows for an opportunity to feel the fullness of your emotions. The paradigm itself acts as a container within which your experience may be allowed to unfold without undue preconditions imposed upon it.

Integrating Spirit

Premise: Synthesis of human experience arrives at a metaphysical singularity of personality extension.

The personality of the physical form is a derivative of many different constructs. One such construct is the astronomical disposition of the celestial mechanics at your time of birth – your astrological character.

If you're open to astrology, the sun-sign is less important than you may realize. In a certain sense, it doesn't exist. That is to say, it's an illusion – a holographic simulation.

If you're not open to astrology, to assume you are not influenced by the celestial bodies that form the entirety of this solar system is an assumption based on an arrogant delusion.

In either case, who you know yourself to be in this world of form has many dispositional factors to consider. Factors you may not have the slightest idea they even exist. Yet, when you arrive at a point of synergy in all your capacities, this form of human expression begins to take on new type of light. Your intellectual light, your physiological light, and your emotional light; these are all aspects of a higher ordered entity that is expressed here *through* the human form.

To constrain your expression to only one avenue is a limitation you impose on yourself. You may have good reason to impose this. For example, out of your concern for the safety of others, you may find significant justification in suppressing anger. As you mature, however, you must begin to refactor this program of anger suppression if you wish to fully know yourself.

Spirit does not exclusively operate in one domain in your expression. Spirit resides as the basis of every domain of your expression in this world. *Spiritual integration* occurs by your choice to move through the disambiguation process. The movements articulated in Article 2 represent an archetype of the various movements that occur in the composition of this symphony. The methods in this Article are a prototype of protocols to begin experimenting with in order to facilitate the progression of the harmonies and melodies of your song – the music of your life. Refactoring these prototypes to your unique song will be required.

Reason alone cannot come to know the fullness of life. Reason can provide clarity regarding what can be known before a choice is made. If there is information that must be gained by an experiment before a conclusion can be reached, reason is the one standing at the doorway of choice – the gatekeeper of Truth.

You are either in charge of your rational process, or a prisoner to it. If you have not tasted the wine, you cannot offer a critique of it. If you have not *fully entered into* the fact of your awareness in the present moment, you cannot rationally deny the power and extent of it. If you deny the depth of the present moment, and its implications for your life, you are likely moving with ignorance, laziness, or both.

The choice to move forward on your journey of full expression is yours alone. No one can do it for you. You move every time you extend willingness to move. Free-will is yours. Own it!

Exercise 1: Breath Integration

Step 1: List all activities in which you can perform the activity of breathing with minimal conscious effort (i.e., brushing teeth, peeing, pooping, preparing certain meals, driving, etc.).

Step 2: Decide to use these activities as ques to breathe more consciously. Construct the intention, that as you start these activities listed, you will first check in with your breath, and take 3 full breaths.

Step 3: During these activities, breathe deeply beginning each inhale by bringing the air into the lower lungs first (using the diaphragm and expanding the belly). The inhale can go back and forth between the upper lungs, and the lower lungs as is comfortable, but begin each breath by moving air toward the diaphragm first. Ensure each breath is comfortably full.

Step 4: Notice the sensations of the body as you move with an awareness of breathing throughout your day.

Step 5: Continue this practice daily for at least 365 days.

Step 6: Notice if your relationship to stress changes over the course of the 365 days.

Step 7: Notice if you begin to construct rationalizations to *not* engage a greater awareness of your breathing. If you allow yourself to rationalize such, be conscious of the justifications you use to discontinue your growth in awareness of your breathing experience, and choose to discontinue. Don't simply allow your habituated rationalization process to dictate your behavior. If you don't wish to continue the practice, choose this for yourself.

NOTE: In any situation you find yourself not needing an intent focus on the task at hand, it is an opportunity to experiment with this practice. Move the intention of your focus to having a greater awareness of your breathing process.

Exercise 2: Body Integration

Step 1: Take three deep breaths in through the nose – **_very_** deep.

Step 2: Hold the 3rd breath for as long as is comfortable.

Step 3: Notice areas in the body where you feel tension, tightness, pain, etc. Holding the breath will help to bring to your awareness these areas.

Step 4: Choose one area of tension and move in a slow dynamic stretch of that area. Use micro-movements to begin the dynamic stretch.

Step 5: Notice if any memories or emotions arise as you begin to release the tension in that area by stretching and breathing.

Step 6: Allow the emotions, memories, insights to flow as you move the body in a dynamic stretch facilitated by deep breathing.

NOTE: The current state of muscle memory in your body is a composition of the entirety of your life experience. You may have locked certain significant emotions into your muscles that you're not aware of at present. This is okay. Be present with your experience of this process as you uncover these buried experiences. If it becomes too intense, seek proper counsel as is necessary to process these experiences in full maturity.

Exercise 3: Mind Integration

Step 1: Research the differences between constructing a literary narrative in 1st person, 2nd person, and 3rd person.

Step 2: Notice the internal dialogue you have with yourself, and in what context the narrative is being composed, 1st, 2nd, 3rd, or a variation thereof.

Step 3: In situations of emotional significance, as you notice yourself in the experience, move to the 3rd person perspective. Being in a silent, safe space may be needed to gain a sense of fluidity with this step. Give yourself the space you need to notice yourself from the 3rd person point-of-view as you feel the fullness of these significant emotions. It does not matter what emotion arises, what matters is neutrally observing your experience. This neutrality is facilitated by the 3rd person point-of-view.

Step 4: Journal your experience. Use any format of journal that is comfortable to you. There is no wrong way to journal. The primary focus is that you put into words your experience of these significant emotions as viewed from the 3rd person.

NOTE: Be careful to not interpret meaning from your experience as you notice yourself. Do not answer the question, "What does this mean" while in the process of noticing yourself. Allow yourself the opportunity to *feel* the significance of the emotion without interpretation of meaning.

Be fully present to witnessing your experiencing of the emotion. There is nothing to do with the emotion. No decisions need to be made while feeling. Simply allow yourself the space to feel it through its full-cycle. If you find it difficult to remain in this space, it is a sign that you may benefit from proper counsel and assistance in the process of feeling the fullness of the emotion. You are not weak to seek assistance.

Seeking the guidance of a mental health professional is often required when dislodging the suppression of intense emotions. Give yourself the opportunity of proper counsel if you notice yourself becoming embroiled in the emotions. And journal! The journaling is the integration. You may draw, paint, or use another creative form if you wish. But the creative expression needs to reflect your noticing of yourself from the 3rd person perspective. Do not use the creative expression as a mechanism of avoidance. Use it as a mechanism of noticing yourself.

Exercise 4: Emotion Integration

Step 1: Take a deep breath and notice yourself in the current experience.

Step 2: Take four more deep breaths as you notice yourself.

Step 3: Begin to describe, out loud, the sensations you feel in your chest, gut, neck, and hands. Do not use similes. Use precise descriptions of the sensation such as hot, cold, big, small, soft, hard, buzzing, tense. Broaden the vocabulary you use to describe your somatic experience. Your sensations don't feel "like" something, they *are* something. Give them the attention they require.

Step 4: Begin to put a label on the emotion you feel in relation to the sensations you described above. For example, if you are feeling tension in the chest, with tightness of the gut, the label that may correlate best is "pensive". Use one-word labels to identify the emotions. Broaden the vocabulary you use to describe your emotional experience. Gather an extensive list of emotions. Your emotions don't feel "like" something, they *are* something. Give them the attention they require.

NOTE: If you notice resistance to this step, and you want to set it aside, this may be the thing that you most need. But it may be that you need to do it with proper counsel. If you notice that you don't feel like doing this exercise, examine the rationalizations being offered by the mind to set this exercise aside. Look for any avoidance. If you notice avoidance, or you feel resistance, go to a mirror, look yourself in the eye, and ask the question, "Why am I avoiding feeling the fullness of my emotions?"

If in response to this question you feel even more resistance arise, acknowledge that you are avoiding something with great significance, and seek proper counsel. Take this exercise to him/her/them, and discuss your experience with it. Allow yourself to get help re-contextualizing your emotional avoidance.

If you identify as a man in this world and you've grown up in a context where "men don't cry", this is even more important. It is likely that assistance in re-programming your consciousness would be advantageous to your processing of life.

You didn't get into this state of avoidance by yourself. There is much in this world that acts as programming to have you avoid. You are not weak to seek out counsel. You are demonstrating weakness to believe you don't need to grow in your emotional maturity. Suppressing emotions for the sake of the *appearance* of being mature without creating space for yourself to process your emotions is not maturity. It is a regression. Childhood is over, and its is time to create opportunity for yourself to grow emotionally.

Exercise 5: Spirit Integration

Step 1: Concentrate your intention toward synergizing the movement of each integration exercise (breath, body, mind, emotion) into one fluid movement.

Step 2: Contemplate the idea of reprogramming your consciousness to a new way of moving in the world. Journal the insight that comes to you.

Step 3: Meditate with the image of an X, Y grid in your mind's eye. The *up* vector indicates mind, the *down* vector indicates emotion, the *right* indicates breath, the *left* indicates body, and the point (0,0) in the center indicates spirit. Place this image in your vision, then come to stillness while engaging the *trinity expression* exercise described in Exercise 3 of Chapter 3 of Article 3.

Step 4: Introspect into all the ways you avoid engaging in a practice of noticing yourself in all of your experiences. Use a mirror to look yourself in the eye and give yourself the opportunity to ask yourself the challenging questions. Face yourself directly. Choose to engage the practice, or choose to not engage it, but don't let your habituated patterns dictate your imprisonment in the cage of ignorance. Choosing to not engage in the practice is a step out of ignorance. Choosing to engage the practice is the beginning of your adventure of self-discovery. This is not a matter of guilt or shame. It is a matter of making a choice for how you intend to live your life. Acknowledging all the ways you hold ignorance as your functional paradigm is part of the ruthless honesty needed to uproot all the ways you deceive yourself. Facing yourself in the mirror is the most direct way to introspect.

Step 5: Repeat Steps 1 through 4 ad infinitum.

Article 4
Truth

The misguided...are dominated by material desires, and consider the attainment of heaven as the highest goal of life. They engage in specific rites for the sake of prosperity and enjoyment. Rebirth is the result of their action. The resolute determination of Self-realization is not formed in the minds of those who are attached to pleasure and power, and whose judgment is obscured by ritualistic activities... The fruits of work should not be your motive, and you should never be inactive. Do your duty to the best of your ability... abandoning worry and selfish attachment to the results, and remaining calm in both success and failure. The selfless service is a yogic practice that brings peace and Happiness of mind. Work done with selfish motives is inferior by far to the selfless service...When your intellect will completely pierce the veil of confusion, then you will become indifferent to what has been heard and what is to be heard from the scriptures. When your intellect, that is confused by the conflicting opinions and the ritualistic doctrine of the Vedas, shall stay steady and firm on concentration of the Supreme Being, then you shall attain union with the Supreme in trance...When one is completely free from all desires of the mind and is satisfied with the Supreme Being by the joy of Supreme Being, then one is called an enlightened person...A person whose mind is unperturbed by sorrow, who does not crave pleasures, and who is completely free from attachment, fear, and anger, is called an enlightened sage of steady intellect...One who abandons all desires, and becomes free from longing and the feeling of 'I' and 'my,' attains peace, this is the super-conscious state of mind. Attaining this state, one is no longer deluded. Gaining this state, even at the end of one's life, a person becomes one with the Absolute.

Bhagavad-Gita 2.41-72

Chapter 1

Yahweh

To Conceive

> If you bring forth what is within you, what you bring forth will save you. If you do not bring forth what is within you, what you do not bring forth will destroy you.
>
> Yeshua

Only insofar as you have sought to understand the premise upon which all existence rests, is the depth to which you have conceived the causal nature of reality. The quest to know God is a quest to be in a relationship with God. And let us call on the function of honesty – *your* concept of God is not God.

No concept of God will ever suffice to understand the Primal Cause of All That Is. Just as no concept by another human will ever suffice to extrapolate an understanding that is You. In order to understand you, one must experience you. In order to experience you, one must be in relationship with you. To conceive of who you are is only the beginning. To further the concept of who you are, one must observe you, be witness to your works, and be a receiver of your light.

To know God is to continually test the concept you have proposed as the Truth of Reality. The word God, in this context, is only a word to speak of that which cannot be contained in a word. And at this point, God may be a meaningless word to you. Or, God may have deep emotional resonance, either with peace, or with anger or some other emotion. The experience you hold in relation to your concept of God is entirely based on *your* concept. This seems redundant. And in a certain context, the redundancy is necessary.

You will never be able to fully *conceive* that which is the prime context for all that exists. But that does not mean you cannot experience an ever-deepening relationship with the fundamental basis of all Life.

The deeper you sense that which holds your existence as a kinetic possibility in this moment, the closer you entwine your conscious heart with the true nature of reality. The Method of *Trinity Expression* in Article 3, Chapter 3 on mediation is designed for exactly this. A question to contemplate as you go is, "have I ever ceased to exist?"

Given that you currently exist, this question may seem trivial, in that the immediate response will probably be 'no'. But let's go a little further. Is it even possible to cease to exist? Sure, the body may die, but do You cease to exist because the body is no longer able to sustain a life current? Does electricity cease to exist because a power plant no longer moves the electrons through a conductive substance?

As you begin to entertain these ruminations, the deeper you go, the more you will begin to see that they all arrive at a more fundamental question – who am I?

Be warned however, this question will become a splinter in your consciousness that may drive you deeper into insanity if you have not wisdom. You are thinking a being – use your powers of reason to deepen your resonant connection to the source of the energetic currents that are sustaining your present existence.

In terms of these energetic currents, it is easy to identify that you are experiencing *an* experience. This much is obvious. It is also easy to identify that you have a capacity to be aware of your awareness. In any moment you recognize that fact that you are observing something, you are in that moment conscious of the fact that you are aware, and by consequence, you are aware that you have life.

And ultimately, this all leads to the point being made – only insofar as you have sought to understand the premise upon which all existence rests, is the depth to which you have conceived the causal nature of reality. But, in this instance, we are speaking of you. Thus, only insofar as You have sought to understand the premise upon which Your existence rests, is the depth to which You have conceived the fundamental reality of who You are.

In any case, whether looking at the macro of all existence, or the micro of your existence, the *basis* is still the same. You are indwelt with life and life is indwelt with you. You cannot speak of "all existence" without considering the fact that you are part of it. So, the question is, who are you?

Chapter 2

Yeshua

An Appeal to Reason

Was Jesus of Nazareth a real person? Is there any empirical proof for this Man that many call upon to be saved by? More importantly, is it absolutely necessary to have empirical proof to be influenced, positively, by the story of the-life-of-the-man known as Yeshua Ben Joseph?

At the heart of these questions is a premise upon which sits a certain justification. This justification implies a great many things if taken in its totality. A justification that; consequently, provides ample reason to lead a life of integrity.

What is this justification?

Certain Christian sects believe that the life of Jesus being slain upon the cross *is* the justification. Others claim that it was his death *and* resurrection. And still others claim that the justification has nothing to do with either of these things.

In any case, the justification speaks to a reality in which all people have been eternally set free by the existence and actions of this one individual.

And if there is to be an appeal to reason, the question must be asked; is it possible? Is it possible for one individual to alter the eternal fate of not only an entire world, but an entire universe?

Empirically speaking, there is no rational proof available to say one way or another. So, in this case, it must be left up to imagination.

In the modern era, there have been examples such as Martin Luther King Jr., and Mahatma Gandhi whose actions have demonstrated that one man can bring about significant positive change on a planet. But still, the implications of these changes are more or less temporal.

The underlying question here is, can the action of an individual fundamentally alter the *eternal* destiny of all people?

And can it be proven as such?

And of equal importance, can it be *disproven* as such?

No. Neither endeavor is possible in the current state of affairs for this world. It is a matter of *faith*. The implication of this is, for any individual who claims to use reason as a guide in life, to either believe *or* disbelieve in that which is the notion of Jesus' life on this planet; reason can neither prove, nor deny it.

The premise that lies at the bottom of all of this is similar to the premise presented at the beginning of this book. And that is, a relationship with Jesus Christ, if possible, is a personal endeavor left to each individual to actively choose to cultivate. It is a freedom given to any individual with a capacity for reason. This degree of faith cannot be dogmatically imposed through the indoctrination of any individual. At some point, the individual must *actively* cultivate the relationship. And thus, the freedom of religion lies in the choice of a sentient being to use reason as a mechanism of thinking, and more importantly, choosing. The freedom herein is inalienable such that it is the derivative of one's ability to use reason in coming to choose what one believes. Only severe forms of brainwashing can strip this freedom from one's power. But again, in any moment, an individual can become aware of awareness, and therein eradicate that mental slavery if one so chooses.

Jesus: The Story

The story of Jesus, as told by the New Testament, contrary to popular belief, is not the most important story being told about Jesus. The single most important story is the one that you are telling yourself.

It matters not if you believe in Jesus, or not. Each is a story that you are actively involved in telling, either by a proactive testimony, or by passive indifference, or a combination thereof.

The premise that underlies the assertions expressed into reality about who you see Jesus as, is a premise that may or may not be true. And ultimately, as has already been discussed, you have no way to prove those assertions as true, or not. The point is, if you hold a story about Jesus that is not true, are you willing to refactor your narrative to illustrate reality more closely?

Meaning, IF you believe that his sacrifice on the cross is what set you free, and in reality, his death has nothing to ultimately do with your salvation, are you willing to let go of the idea that his death was a necessary ingredient in your salvation? And if you're not willing to revise that idea, you might consider that you are prone to worshipping a false notion in place of the truth – an idol.

Likewise, IF you believe it's not possible for one individual to forever alter the spiritual destiny of an entire universe, and it in fact is possible, are you willing to revise your belief and line up with the reality being offered as an answer to spiritual stagnation? And if you're not willing to revise that idea, you might consider that you are resisting your own happiness.

The story of Jesus, whether of belief, or disbelief, is a story that only you can tell. Others give testimony, yes. But it's not their testimony that holds the key to the truth of Jesus. It is your testimony you are narrating to yourself. You can start with the gospels, but it cannot stop there. Who is Jesus in your present tense experience?

If you believe Jesus is a real entity whom you can experience a real relationship with, what are you doing to cultivate that relationship now? If you believe Jesus is only a story concocted and there is no basis of a real entity underlying the story, does the story hold any value in terms of living a life more in alignment with reality?

Fundamentally, you cannot escape the fact that the story of Jesus influences you. By the fact that you are thinking about such things, the influence is at work. Will you use the story to influence your situation to the benefit of yourself and others, or will you use the story in other ways?

Jesus: The Man

Of what character is a man who believes in something so strong that he is willing to be tortured, and hung on cross in testimony of what he believes? Aside from the idea that Jesus is the savior of mankind, who is the Man known as Yeshua ben Joseph?

Let's assume for a moment that Yeshua was a living breathing human. Let's also provide an accurate context for that as well by saying he was a man, as any man. A man facing his humanness as any other man faces his humanness.

What line of thinking, and what series of decisions did he make that led him to his ultimate fate. Was his line of thinking, that he was the Son of the Creator of all things, an accurate line of thinking? And if it was accurate, what implications did that have on his humanness?

Assuming he had the powers of reason as any sentient being does, what premise underlies his reasoning such that he was able to live a life that is still known today? Has there been any other figure, real or fictional, as influential as the man known as Jesus? Perhaps, Buddha, Krishna, Moses, and even Muhammad. But then again, let's look at the single most printed book in the world – the Bible – one third of which is dedicated to the life and ideas of the man known as Jesus.

Assuming that Jesus was a real, living, breathing, burping, peeing, pooping, farting man, what does it say about his influence in this world, such that the story of his life is the single most published story in history? Would you care to be so influential?

Imagine you held a premise with such power, that your actions in the world became the gospel for billions of people over thousands of years. What would that premise have to be?

Jesus: The Messiah

It is written in the gospels that Jesus said, "I Am the Light of the World, he who follows me shall not walk in darkness, but have the light of life" (John 8:12). It's also written that Jesus said, "You are the light of the world...let your light so shine before men, that they may see your good works and glorify your Father in heaven" (Matthew 5:14).

If you were to research the etymology of the word "Messiah" you would come to a notion of it being related to being "anointed". And over time, the meaning transformed into the notion of a "savior" who was expected to set free a people whom were being held captive.

The question is, do you believe?

Ultimately, only you can answer that question. And it matters not what you say, it only matters what you hold to be true in your heart. Only you can reason for yourself. If you give up that power, you abdicate that which transports you to your freedom.

If you do believe, do you hold yourself accountable to the standards of living in the discipline of a Christ-like nature? Do you know what those standards are? Have you examined the premise articulated by Jesus, and found it to be a valid premise? By what mechanism have you found it to be valid?

If Jesus is your savior, what have you implemented in your life that stands as an expression of your salvation? Do you pretend to be saved by only entertaining the mental construct of being a Christian, or do you actually live an inner-life worthy of being considered a Christ; an anointed disciple of the Most High?

Do you actually love your neighbor as yourself? Do you actually love yourself? And going even deeper, do you love the source of your life with all of your strength, all of your mind, all of your heart, and all of your soul?

Or do you hold closets of tendencies that degrade your capacity to open yourself to the living waters of Life's most sacred fountain?

You can fool yourself for only so long. Eventually, your deceit will be the demise of you. The journey of moral perfection will, by necessity, drive you to the deepest darkest parts of yourself. What you do in those moments, when you find the lights have gone out will determine whether you actually love with all that is your Self. Anything less is only an indication that you have more work to do.

Jesus: The Christ

Christ, the nature of divine Sonship. The Christ character; a universal disposition of divine birthright. All souls are destined to embrace the universality of the Christed order.

Christ, the universal disposition, is a *way of being* and is open to all individuals who shall wish to know Truth by living according to its divine injunction. And although all are destined to this divine reconciliation, every individual must actively work out their own path toward that end, which never actually ends. As such, the journey here in the present is the destination. The beginning and the end meet right here in this moment.

This universal journey is an eternal adventure of an infinite degree that travels through all domains for the purpose of extending the currents of life's source energy.

Divine Grace is the integral characteristic of the Christed nature. Initiation of this order is entering into a state of divine nobility, and only those who are dedicated to the Prime Creator's universal decrees can enter this degree of nobility.

It is not merely a mental pursuit. The transformation involved in donning the armor of divine nobility is total and complete recognition of the essential nature of reality through all aspects of one's being. Here on earth, that recognition travels through ones mental, emotional, physical and spiritual makeup.

To be guided in all ways by the coordinating actions of the Creator's universal decree is to be guided by the Chief Guide of the Eternal Son and the Eternal Spirit. Together, this trinity establishes Christ, the character of divine personality.

The moment of choice to travel this journey of facing this revelation is now.

Chapter 3

You

Ego

> If those who lead you say, 'See the Kingdom is in the sky,' then the birds of the sky will precede you. If they say to you, 'It is in the sea,' then the fish will precede you. Rather, the Kingdom is inside of you, and it is outside of you. When you come to know yourselves, then you will become known, and you will realize that it is you who are the children of the living Creator. But if you will not know yourselves, you dwell in poverty, and it is you who are that poverty.
>
> Yeshua

Who are you? Take a moment to notice what arises in your mind as you ponder this simple question. For the moment, just allow your mind to produce whatever narrative arises. There is no need to control the story for this exercise. Simply allow the story to reveal itself.

As the narrative arises, begin to notice where you sense an increase in emotionality. Sense the fluctuations in the emotion as you peruse the identity of You. The narrative may drift back to a time when you were a child, or it may be of a more recent scene.

The narrative may also speak of various philosophical underpinnings. Does it show more of a humanist orientation? Or does if tend toward more of a spiritual? Does the narrative invoke religious undertones, for example, does it caste you as a sinner, born of corruption as the basis of your existence? Or does what you are seeing arise paint you as a perfect rendition of the Creator's impeccable perfection?

Before continuing on, take a few minutes to perform this exercise if you have not already done so. You may be thinking that you have done similar exercises in the past, and that you understand the purpose of the exercise, and thereby do not necessarily need to do it. And you are correct; you do not *need* to do it. However, consider that all the times you have done a similar exercise in the past, it revealed to you the narrative pertaining to you in that moment. Here, in the present, you are at a different place. What arises now will be based on the totality of your experience here.

Assuming that you have taken the time to call forth the context of the narrative that is here for you in the present, it can be used as input for the remainder of this chapter. As you continue, begin to increase awareness of your somatic experience. Sense your body and your emotions. Put greater emphasis on the awareness of these aspects of yourself while keeping in mind the context of the narrative of who you are.

What aspects of the narrative are you unwilling to let go of? Are you a parent of a young children that you are committed to seeing them through their growth into adulthood? What emphasis do you place on your role as mother or father? Is this an aspect of your narrative that you are unwilling to remove from the story of who you are?

Notice the emotion that arises as you ponder these questions. For some, the idea may arise that it's ridiculous to even consider such a surrender of that type of role. And that feeling of resistance may be so strong that it acts as an impetus to discontinue reading. If you are a parent, notice if this is the case for you. Do you have an experience of decreasing the importance of continuing to read? Are there rationalizations arising that would have you protect your view of things such that you're not even willing to consider the idea of letting go of this aspect of your personal narrative? Simply notice yourself.

Maybe you don't have children. What in your life is the single most important thing you do on a regular basis? What do you value above all else? Are you willing to let go of that aspect of your personal narrative? Notice yourself as you ponder the possibility of letting go of the single most important thing in your life. What sensations arise in your body? What feelings arise in your emotions? What rationalizations arise in your mind to justify your unwillingness to surrender this most important thing in your life? Simply notice yourself.

Be careful here, do not assume that you *have* to be willing to let go of it. This is simply an exercise of noticing yourself. If the exercise is too intense, and you wish to take some space, the choice to honor yourself in the way that you feel is best for you is yours alone. Do what you feel is best for you.

If you're still here, and you have not felt a resonance of difficulty, you are likely only allowing yourself to do this exercise at a surface level. If you wish to fully face yourself, you are encouraged to rest here with the exercise until you have found that one thing that is above all else before continuing. When you have found that thing then consider the idea of letting it go.

If you do this exercise with a significant degree of sincerity, you will have no choice but to feel the difficulty. You have already made a choice by doing the exercise. The following contemplations are here as a method of revealing a doorway to view things from a higher perspective.

Assuming you are still present to your unwillingness to let go of that which calls to you as one of the single most important values of your life, what would happen tomorrow if you ceased breathing tonight?

If your life ended, would that aspect of your personal narrative still pertain to your individual experience?

If the person you were in this world was no more, who would act as the entity giving importance to the aspect of your personal human narrative that you are unwilling to surrender?

Do you believe your future physical existence is guaranteed?

What emotions are present as you contemplate this context? Notice yourself. Is there anxiety, or paranoia? Is there fear, concern, worry, doubt? Dissect the emotional resonance you are experiencing.

Who Am I

Attachment to personal narrative acts as a basis for the ego to influence decisions. This is neither right nor wrong; neither good nor bad. It is simply a function of being human.

Identifying *self* as the character in the personal narrative creates the ego. As a human, this process of identifying self as the character in the personal narrative cannot be circumvented. It is part of the human experience. Being aware of the identification process; however, allows for decisions that are influenced by a transcendent paradigm, or higher perspective.

Isolating the character of who you are to an impermanent basis of identity will undoubtedly lead to existential paranoia. In simple terms, you do not know yourself when the basis of your identity is founded on a temporal narrative.

Knowing yourself in fullness requires the cessation of all attachments to a temporal identity. This does not mean that you cannot play the role of parent. Indeed, playing the role of a parent can act as the single most effective method for the ceasing of attachment to temporal identity. This may seem like a paradox. It is only paradoxical insofar as your identity is *based* on the role you play. *Not* playing a role in life is *not* possible. By the fact of existing, a role is being played. Identifying oneself *as* that role is a misconception.

As a parent, you will come to face all that which is unresolved about your childhood. You have no choice for it to present itself to you. That choice dissipated at the intersection of sperm and egg. As a parent, you can *try* to ignore that which is unresolved in you from your childhood, but it will likely require some kind of chemical stimulant to do so. Furthermore, you will likely fail at ignoring your unresolved past, even if you're not a parent. When the pain and turmoil of your present life overwhelms you, it is in that moment when a decision for resolution can be enacted. Seek the help you need to see yourself through it. You are not alone.

Chapter 4

Reclaiming the Earth

The Life of a Rastafarian Druid: Spreading the Love

In the simplicity of love there is only one thing to *do* – LOVE! The intention surmounts to being a generating agent of the most basic life force available to all of existence. There need be no other reason or motivation to love than *to love*. Loving that which is present in every moment, in the face of what may act contrary to being present to love, comes with it liberation. Resistance to this indicates resistance to accepting *un*conditional love as the basis of reality.

It is not a journey that the intellectual mind will comprehend until the intellectual mind is allowed to integrate into a Mind beyond current comprehension. It is; however, a journey that the heart will immediately understand because *it is a journey that is navigated by the heart*.

Reconcile that which holds you back from dwelling in a Love that is transcendent of obstacles. This love is currently washing through you. Be still and you can sense its presence in the vibrations of your being. The journey of reconciliation is embracing the presence of this love with every breath. The pre-requisite is a willingness to take the journey.

All space, and all matter in space, resonates as a representation of that which is the foundation of all existence. Refining perceptual capacities to a clear point of observation is the key that starts the engine of the vehicle that will move you on this journey. There is no need to label what is perceived before being *aware* of its existence. Allow the awareness of its existence to exist as it is before compartmentalizing the experience with language.

Notice the sensing activity that is currently taking place in the body. Feel the lungs fill with air, then deflate. Hear all sounds, do not put a label on the sounds, such as "oh, that's just a little birdy on my windowsill;" but rather, notice the vibrations of the sounds as they resonate in the body.

From this sensing space, move the attention point into the center of the chest. Breathe deep and slow, through the nose.

Feel the chest as the air moves through the passages and chambers that facilitate the movement of air in the body. Feel the blood purifying itself and then pumping through the circulatory system with every pulse of the heart. Exhale all the waste and eliminate it from the body.

Sense the body.

From this space *to love* is only a choice away. A decision to frame an intention to be a capacitor of this energy. The next step is to hold the heart in a space of willingness. Intend for it to wash All that is in you in the purity that sits as the singularity of your existing spiritual construct.

In every moment of perception, this base intention of willingness is the keystone that holds the doorway of heaven open for divinity to move through you – and radiate all existence with divine energy.

The space all around us is an infinite holomorphic fractal that is permeating with energy in every layer of its construction. In the most infinitesimally small structure in the universe, the entirety of the infinitely large universe is contained. This is the paradox of the Sacred Instant. And in this is the reality of the singularity that sits at the basis of *your* existence; you are the light of the world.

In the moment that these words are being read, there exists an Entity that is composed entirely of this universe. Its physical body is composed of stardust, and its awareness is sourced as a singularity of an infinite framework of embodiment.

Existence exists. This axiomatic fact is the basis of all rational perception; that is, observing reality in the present. Misperception and misconception arise from straying away from this point of focus. This focal point involves the mind, the heart, and the body; the three units of simultaneous human expression.

In this paradigm of living, it is assumed that the soul is an active participant in life. As the soul is the spiritual foundation, the metaphysical archetype, for the existence of the physical human body. **Without** the electromagnetic life force coursing through the body, the body is a rotting corpse. **With** the electromagnetic life force, the body is active and vibrant in the expression of life.

Fostering Love occurs with a choice: to *currently* perceive all life as a movement of this life force.

Move with a clear space of intent in the spiritual energy fields of consciousness that is human experience. Doing so will allow all life to freely radiate its full radiance *in you*. Perceiving through biased filters skews perception and is the beginning of judgment.

Breathe deep. Sense the whole body. Resonate the implicit gratitude emanating throughout the entirety of this moment.

This *movement* clears judgment from the energy fields. And it reveals where there are attachments that act as restrictions to the flowing nature of the energy permeating the fields of space all around us.

Transmuting all stagnant energy and purifying the interpenetrating energy fields is a pathway toward a healthier paradigm. From this state of health, a space-of-love can be established as a *way-of-living*; wherein, the active environment held as one's *way of being* is the predefined context for others to exist inside of; that is, *loving your neighbor as yourself*.

Chapter 5

Becoming The Christ

The Indwelling

Let's do an exercise by following a line of questions. These questions are a binomial experiment in that they are only answered with one of two possible answers – Yes, or No. Notice if, throughout this process, you tend to resist this thought experiment.

Are you aware?

Are you living (is life-activity animating your physical construct)?

Are you free to continue reading these words?

Are you able to become aware of your breathing process?

Do you have a sense-perception of your body?

All the questions are meant to be answered with a Yes. If you have answered 'no' to any of them, I invite you to go back to the question(s) you answered 'no' to and contemplate the question further.

In the fact that you have answered yes to these questions, is the presupposition that you have the ability to *reconcile* your life. Meaning, you are aware of the fact that you are alive with a freedom to choose to become increasingly *aware* of how *you* experience your life. And with that, you are free to choose *how* you experience your life.

If you missed the subtle distinction of those last two sentences, please, re-read them again. Grasping the distinction is critical to understanding the fact that you are indwelt with the ability to be an active participant in life.

Active participation in the experience of life resolves to the root of *how*. As you move in that resolution of the root-cause of suffering in your experience, you will most assuredly come to face delusions you've constructed to keep your sense of self "safe". In other words, you will, at some point, come to face existential anxiety. At this juncture, the paranoia of not knowing who you are can easily take you further into insanity if you have not proper guidance. You are *not* who you think you are. You are much more than that. Re-read and contemplate the last paragraph of the *Inroads* at the beginning of this book, if you notice yourself with question.

Forgiveness

A stagnant pond breeds disease. Flowing water breeds a vibrant bio-diversity. Stagnancy results from blockages in a system. Inasmuch as stagnant water can be refreshed by an inflow of new water, and an outflow of the old water, so too can the stagnant energy in the bio-spiritual human construct be refreshed with newness. The *refresh* process is forgiveness.

Holding onto resentment, in any form, creates blockages in the system. Resentment may present itself as anger, fear, regret, or a plethora of other emotions. Yet, at the base of all that is a sentiment that establishes the narrative perpetuating the feedback loop of emotion; this is re-sentment. The only one that is playing an active role in that process is the one who experiences the emotions regarding a particular experience. Holding this resonant energy confined inside the bio-spiritual construct is, in effect, a method to hold the energy stagnant.

Resentment is an active process of building emotional blocks in the bio-spiritual structure. A damming of flowing waters in your soul. A damning of your experience. A curse on yourself. Disease, in some form, is surely to follow.

Cultivating a willingness to shift the perspective of the situation is the single most important decision to make. Attachment to the mental construct of the perspective establishing resent does not allow for willingness. The simple movement of *considering* that there may be a fuller context of the situation is itself cultivating willingness. The vulnerability required in this process is what allows the heart to shift its basis to a more stable position. Accountability is not the same as forgiveness. Full accountability is not in your control. In situations involving others, accountability requires involving others to varying degrees of engagement. Forgiveness is in your full control. Contemplate the distinction if you have these two movements conflated.

In this process, the trap of seeking retribution and/or accountability on the part of others may not lead to forgiveness. Reconciliation is not forgiveness. Reconciliation involves forgiveness. Forgiveness, herein defined, is a process wholly contained within the bio-spiritual structure of the individual. The effects of the process transcend the individual, but the full execution of the function of forgiveness is based entirely on the decisions of the one who forgives.

Everliving Freedom

Ever unfolding the eternally infinite disposition of the sacred heart into all aspects of existence is the movement of the algorithmic function of true freedom. Guidance moves by allocating grace to every spark of divine individuality. Every sentient being is a spark of that which supplies the ever-emerging sustenance of simultaneous cosmic potential.

The spark of this infinite intelligence is placed at the center of an individual's being – the heart. From this point-of-origin the coordinate movements array outward in infinite degrees of potential, creating a sphere of activity in which all possibilities for that individual exist. In every moment, the origin point is ever present.

The origin on a three-dimensional grid system is notated by (0,0,0). The trinitized zero point establishes a reiterating triangular orientation, three axis lines, three origin points, and a space in which activity can take place. This is the initial and primal frame of reference for every individual.

One axis line is one dimensional, giving rise to two directions, left and right. Two axis lines is two dimensional, giving rise to four directions, left/right and up/down. Three axis lines is three dimensional, giving rise to six directions, left/right, up/down, and front/back. Three axis lines also gives rise to a sphere. Putting that sphere into motion gives rise to a fourth dimension – choice!

Chapter 6

The Fallacy of Religion

Loving Yourself

Religion, in its modern convention [circa 2022], has a legitimacy that is questionable at best. Acting as a dispensation of divine interpretation for the masses, a preacher giving alterations to the social conventions of "loving your fellow man" while in the same breath denigrating oneself to a worthless and despicable bag of flesh, relates in no-way to the premise of "being made in the image likeness". If you have this type of notion in your thinking strategy, it would be highly favorable to your experience to refactor it immediately.

If the first premise of divine love is to "love God with all your heart, mind, soul and strength", then the presumption is that the soul is the basis for the capacity of such a magnitude. No viable magnitude exists for one who does not have a functionally conscious relation with the present moment.

Thinking that humanity is contemptible necessarily predisposes the mind toward such fallacies as that proposed by modern religions – that sin is real. Indeed, sin is real, insofar as the one who beseeches others to "love your fellow man" but hate yourself.
It is not possible to simultaneously hold in the mind the conception of the individual being inherently sinful, while also holding to the idea of being able to love another in the fullness of first magnitude. One idea is a violation of the validity of the other. Loving another because of the weaknesses that are presumed to be inherent to a soul is a preemptive attack on the idea that a soul is made in the "image and likeness".

Either you love God by establishing the esteem of being made in the image and likeness as a predicate to your operating constitution, or you don't. You cannot love God if you waiver in your love for yourself. You cannot love others if you do not love the *fact* of your existence.

Be warned, however, against the false notions of self-love. The image of yourself in your mind should never be the predicate of your love for God, yourself, or others. The moment you love the image of yourself that you hold in your mind **as** yourself, you are, in effect, denigrating yourself to a false-notion. Be not futile in your attempts to live according to your true nature.

Holding true to the premise that a soul is composed as an expression of the conception of God obviates the necessity to destroy all notions of depravity in oneself. It is not possible for self-denigration to lead to the loving of God. One cannot love God while simultaneously hating any individual – especially oneself.

In that same vein, it is not possible to love God while idolizing oneself. To come to know God is to fully understand oneself, as there is no separation between the two.

A belief in God as conceived by the mind is not necessary so long as an individual has the capacity to accept the fact of existing in present time; the heart is the central focal point. In the complete acceptance of your existence is the acceptance of the full nature of God; understanding follows.

The images composed in the vast reaches of your mind are images of your own construction and act as models of reality. The image composed by *That Which* stands as the substance of everything exists as an objective fact in reality. One image is real, the other is so helplessly not.

The *Image and likeness* that exists as objective fact need only look at the ability to be aware of these words for the proof of the objective fact. The empirical nature of these observations is made plain insofar as a conscious effort to recognize your ability to observe is fostered.

Religion fails when the focus is taken away from the objective fact of an individual's existence as an *extension* of the primal cause of all reality. Religion succeeds insofar as the individual is brought into a clearer conception of the reality of existing. Direct experience is the vehicle of this clarification process.

Condemning others to the prescriptive analysis of your own judgment, by necessity, condemns yourself to that same judgment. Sin, by its nature, is only possible insofar as you see a separation from the unequaled prime-ness of your source. The origin of your soul cannot be divided. A singularity is whole and complete without equivocation.

Chapter 7

Union through Sex

For the Mathematicians Among Us

Eight coordinate-points are used to establish a graph of vector trajectories in the composition of this particular configuration of union. This configuration is not a sequence or linear progression. Rather, it is 8 points of a graph encompassing an intense level of energy; wherein, the activation of this energy state happens as an aligning of one's intentional matrix with the intentional matrix of a *consenting* partner; A ∪ B.

Consent, the absolute requirement in this movement. Without it, union is not possible. The *intention* of full consensual interaction is the required parameter when calling the union(*consent*)[8] function.

The configuration is as follows.

1) I want to desire her spirit, soul, mind, body
2) I want to be desired by her spirit, soul, mind, body.
3) I want her to want to desire my spirit, soul, mind, body.
4) I want her to want to be desired by my spirit, soul, mind, body.
5) She wants to desire my spirit, soul, mind, body
6) She wants to be desired by my spirit, soul, mind, body.

---

[8] The syntax denoted here in this sentence is best understood by researching the basics of *functions* as used in software. There is a function 'union( )' that requires input in order for it to work. That input is a parameter 'consent'. In this example, it is saying that union is not possible without consent. The function of union needs consent in order for it to work. If consent is not present, the compiler will throw an error. A "bug".

7) She wants me to want to desire her spirit, soul, mind, body.

8) She wants me to want to be desired by her spirit, soul, mind, body.

These desires cross correlate. It may seem that, for example, coordinate three and five are saying the same thing. If you look from the perspective of ownership of the desire, however, the subtle distinction will appear. Coordinate three is my desire, and five is hers.

Moving the intensity of the energetic space created by this *psychical-spiritual* context, up into the heart then begins to enter a domain of love that supersedes all other forms. Remember, *consent* is the absolute upon which this union rests.

Beginning with sex, and the inherent capacity to feel desire, is a doorway to beginning the practice of a supreme form of consensual love. Physical sex is, however, not the end goal.

The practicing of this type of love enters a state of perfection as each partner enters into this configuration with the fullness of mutual consent; wherein, there is no obligation on either party that acts as an expectation on the other. The consent is of pure volition.

The *basis* of the relational vibratory pattern exists as a cultivation of space. First in the centering of oneself in the heart, and further refined by the expansions of orgasmic potential in the creative force of sex. Establishing this configuration can then elevate the capacity of the primal manifolds of one's physical reality and connect it to a cosmic energy structure of individual conscious awareness that transcends the bounds of human separation – Unity.

The pre-requisite needed to enter into this state is a capacity for emotional intelligence. A maturity in emotions that operates the function to acknowledge the depth of desire present in the orgasmic state. Meaning, as an orgasm is beginning to climax, the responsibility required is such that one must be able to respect the revocation of consent by the other party in an instant. In other words, if, for example, a man is on the verge of orgasm, and the woman, for whatever reason, revokes consent, the man must be able to be with the intensity of his experience such that he does not force his desire in or on her. Neither must he blame her nor shame her in any form for not continuing. If the woman is not in full consent of being engaged, the man must possess an emotional quotient that has the capacity to respect the decision of the woman. The same is true if the role of revoking consent is reversed. A woman must respect the man in the same capacity of emotional maturity.

Only at the doorway of the consensual space of supreme respect can the honor of a higher-level love manifest. Integrity is the absolute.

The analogy used above is typified as a relation between heterogeneous pairs. The internal space outlined can also be activated between homogenous pairs. Gender and biological sex are inconsequential to the consensual forming on this union. The internal state of the individuals engaged is the primary directive allocating the energetic configuration. A space wherein the degree-of-attention, and intention, brought to bear by each individual coalesces the energetic intensity fueling the potential elevation.

> At the resurrection people will neither marry nor be given in marriage; In this respect they will be like the angels in heaven.
>
> Yeshua

Additionally, this configuration is only possible between two individuals. There are 8 coordinate-points to the pattern that constructs this mechanism of energy. Poly-relational type engagements requires a significantly more complex graph to be able to reach the same energy state. An energy state that is efficiently possible by two individuals wholly committed to each other.

This is not to say that poly-relational configurations are an inherently invalid form of expressing love. This is saying, however, that those types of arrangements are of a greater complexity. As such, it requires the proper attention of each individual in the relation to come to agreement with every other individual in the arrangement. The level of consensual connection described above by the eight points must be established by all in the poly-configuration. A full integration of honesty in the configuration is an absolute requirement. It cannot be circumvented in any way.

If anyone in a poly-relational configuration has any reservations, the energy state created can only ascend to the manifold capacity of the one with the reservation. A chain is only as strong as its weakest link. That is not to say that the individual is weak, but that anyone with a reservation must have the self-respect to honor the boundary, and the others must be of an emotional maturity to respect the reservation; decisions must then be made at that juncture.

The same is true of relationships between two individuals, of course, but with two individuals there are only two edges to the graph. Between three individuals there are six edges. Between four, 12 edges. The addition of another individual is another layer of complexity wherein all parties must be okay with all other parties having the choice to desire and love any other individual in the configuration of the same accord.

Acknowledgement of preference toward one individual or another must be openly acknowledged with all others. Nothing can remain hidden in the space of absolute love. By uniting in this type of configuration, a distinct emotional maturity in the individuals is an absolute requirement. It will not be a clear space otherwise.

Monogamous relationships offer parsimony. Insofar as each individual is *willing* to face and feel all that stands in the way of full transparency with another, is the degree of potential the relational space holds as the resonant capacity for ascension (i.e., growth/maturity). Poly-amorous, polygamous, or polyandry relationships require the same degree of transparency between individuals, but with increased complexity of the configuration being created.

If being in a relationship typified by the supreme form of love is truly the goal, committed monogamous relational structures offers the surest and simplest path to purify the heart that is required by the ascension. If the desire is more centered in the lower energy vortices, the intention is shifted by a range away from purifying and elevating the energy of the heart; and as such, it must be recognized that supreme love is not really the goal in that case.

Acknowledgment of this fact is necessary for one who wishes to grow on the path of life. Else, the non-acknowledgment is merely a form of self-deceit acting as a block to one's personal growth. Little growth will come until this block is faced and rectified. Cultivating a willingness to fully open to the honesty required to exist in the freedom of transparent self-expression is what is needed. And herein is an opportunity to instantiate the algorithm of freedom. The decision is left to the one reading these words.

Chapter 8

On {this} Philosophy

For the Philosophers Among Us

Obviously, this rendition of a philosophy has its issues. All philosophies expressed in written form do. In this case, there are logical assertions in here that take great leaps of reasoning to approach the conclusion. The point of this dissertation is not to have a pristine logical framework that cannot be dissected. The point is quite different in fact.

Take every instance to dissect this work and fully contemplate the considerations thereof. Be sure to approach the contemplation without preconceived notions, however. Come to them with a fresh mind, free of both intellectual and emotional baggage.

Conversely, do not accept what is said here as the whole truth and nothing but the truth. Understand that as an author, I have my own baggage that I'm working to undo as I write this. And that is the whole point of the philosophy; the undoing of baggage such that I can more fully face the Revelation of my heart herein this instant. No one person has an impeccably expressed character.

This book has been through an 11-year creation process, and three major revisions. Not one single sentence from that first version remains in this final version. In that same vein, this book has seen my personal journey progress through being a single man responsible only to myself, to a husband and father of five, to being separated from my family due to my inability to be responsible with my emotions. Needless to say, some intense and massive paradigms shifts have taken place during the course of writing this book. In many ways, the writing of this book, and others has been a form of therapy I have had heavy reliance on.

At the end of the day, I have a human experience just like you, and am only seeking to offer my perspective on life. I write this book for the sole purpose of benefiting both my life as well as other people's lives. Through the course of writing this book, and applying the principles espoused herein to my own life, I have come to reap some of the benefits of this thinking strategy.

Do I sometimes fall flat on my face? Of course. And it hurts too. But the point is to get back up and keep walking. And hopefully next time, if I've given proper attention to my experience, I'm not so blind as to what caused me to previously fall. If I'm going to fail, I'd prefer to fail fast, in small ways, and learn from it such that major and harmful mistakes can be avoided.

If you find yourself wanting to debate the premises and assertions contained herein you can find someone else to debate them with. I have no desire to *prove* these things to anyone. For me, much of what is contained herein is self-evident for someone who proactively applies the scientific method to one's own thinking, feeling, and experiencing. Meaning, I actively desire to be shown all the ways my thinking is wrong. In such a way, I can more effectively remove the baggage from my life. I do not, however, wish to engage in a debate of whether the fundamental premise is valid or not – its validity is self-evident. If you don't see this "self-evidence" I cannot show it to you, nor can I provide the logic for you to see it if you are not willing to let irrational skepticism rest. As has been said throughout, *direct experience* is the only possible place where this "self-evidence" is available. You're the only one who can generate willingness to move beyond your skepticism. That is your charge.

Willingness to let go of that which you think you know is the mirror you must face, and ultimately use to exit the matrix of your ideology that has you suffer. Do not delude yourself by thinking you are suffer-free. Check in with your body, do you experience a pain-point on a residual basis?

That said, although I have no desire to debate this thinking strategy, I have a great desire to refactor it according to concepts that have proven to be more effective toward the purpose of loving life and the living of it.

Please, by all means, test this strategy. Find what works for you and your situation. Leave the rest for later.

At the end of the day, this is my best attempt to articulate my personal philosophy on life. I do not expect you to adopt this as your own. But I do expect that you are **actively engaged** in formulating your own. If not, I encourage you to do so. My hope is that you will find a piece or two contained herein that brings efficacy to your experience.

May contentment and joy fill your heart.

Other Titles by Michael Phoenix

Visit https://MichaelPhoenix.me for more.
- "Of the First Magnitude" series
    - Facing Revelation: An Emerging
    - Quantum Engineering: Introspecting the Rabbit Hole
    - Algorhythmic Insight: Poetic Analysis of the Journey
- Body Integration & the One Minute Workout: Learning to Love the Body You're In
- "On Eros" series
    - Cōnsēnsiō: On the Bedrock of Consent
    - Sēnsuālitās: The Fountain of Sensual Experience
    - Sublīmātiō: The Serpent of Elevating Embodiment

Of The First Magnitude

~I~

~Volume 1~
Facing Revelation
An Emerging

~Volume 2~
iRise
An Algorhythm of Freedom

~Volume 3~
Quantum Engineering
Introspecting the Rabbit Hole

~Volume 4~
Algorhythmic Insight
Poetic Analysis of the Journey

www.ingramcontent.com/pod-product-compliance
Lightning Source LLC
Chambersburg PA
CBHW031438160426
43195CB00010BB/769